MW01107203

CONTENTS

Chapter 1.	1
Chapter 2.	20
Chapter 3.	42
Chapter 4.	56
Chapter 5.	60
Chapter 6.	71
Chapter 7.	79
Chapter 8.	91
Chapter 9.	96
Chapter. 10	101

I WOULD LIKE TO GIVE THANKS
TO EVERY SINGLE STAFF FROM
THE ENGLISH DEPARTMENT AT
NASHOBA REGIONAL HIGH SCHOOL.
IT'S BECAUSE OF THESE SPECIAL
TEACHERS THAT I WAS ABLE TO
FIND MY TALENT IN WRITING TO
EXPRESS MYSELF, AND PURSUE IT
TO UNIMAGINABLE HEIGHTS. WHILE
ALL ODDS WERE AGAINST ME, YOU
GUYS SHOWED ABUNDANT CARE AND
SUPPORT. THAT WAS ALL THE PUSH
I NEEDED TO GAIN MY CONFIDENCE
AND MOVE FOWARD. THIS IS THE
START OF SOMETHING GREAT AND YOU
GUYS ARE DEFINETLY PART OF IT.

"If there is a book that you want to read, but it hasn't been written yet, you must be the one to write it." -Toni Morrison

CHAPTER 1.

"Look who's here"

"**H**ey, be easy on my head. I want my hair done neat, but that don't mean ripping my head off while doing so. I knew I should've asked Mikah instead," I shouted at my sister.

"Okay, go ask her to do it then. I'm doing you a favor and you want to be so rude," Djeny slammed the comb on the table and stood up.

"It's just you have heavy hands, that's all."

But Djeny was already walking into the other room, and here I was looking silly with my hair half done. I got up and ran to the bathroom. I stared at the mirror as I teased myself. Half of my hair was braided into cornrows, and the other half was into a bun that was tied with a knot. Now I just needed to get somebody to help me finish up this mess on my head. I knew Djeny wasn't going to help out since I pissed her off. I could ask Mikah but she was in the middle of her favorite show, and she would bug out on me if I interrupted her. Tati, who is my aunt, was in the kitchen getting dinner ready, so she couldn't help out much. Even with the doors closed you could still smell the food as if it was being made right in front of you. The smell of her cooked meals used to make my stomach rumble as if an earthquake was happening.

way through the afternoon. Late in the afternoon he would make stops at the office and was always on the move. I would sit around for him while he talked on the phone but I would get bored so I'd run back upstairs.

Climbing up the stairs to the third floor was a big drag. The stairs were really big to me at the time. It was like going up a 3 story building. My dad lived and worked on the second floor, so he had about half of the stairs I had to climb. The first floor of the house was being rented out to close friends of my dad. I never saw them much,they were just 2 working couples who were close, and strong supporters of my dad. But lucky them they didn't have to go up so many stairs.

In the living room with Mikah, I got caught up in the television show we were watching. The drama of the show took up all my attention. I wanted to question Mikah about getting my hair done, but for the moment it didn't bother me. At the end of the day I knew it would get done; otherwise my aunt would get upset.

It was just past noon. The day was bright and I could hear the life of the city going on outside; cars honked, chickens sung, people shouted and kompa, slow haitian music- blasted from speakers on the street. The doorbell rang. I quickly jumped to my feet and ran to the window to see who it was. It was really rare that we got company.

"Go sit your butt somewhere boy!" Tati demanded.

I went on and did as she ordered. It was always a hassle to go open the doors anyway. Since the house was 3 floors, we would have to go all the way to the first floor, which for me felt like a mile of stairs. I stood by the window looking down, filled with curiosity wanting to know who was there.

A couple minutes later Tati walked up, and behind her stood my mom. I stood opposite of her feeling a lot of different emotions. In my head I was really surprised to see her; in my heart I felt this warm and filled feeling seeing her here. I was happy, shocked, sad, and glad all at the same time. I quickly ran to her and gave her a hug.

"Rose! hi! When did you--? Are you staying?"

It's as if I was learning to talk again. Rosett is my mom's first name. I found it better to call her "Rose" for short . Rose sounded better than "mom." but she was fine with it and so was I. About a minute went by and i was still holding on to her. I started to tear up but it was more tears of joy rather than sad tears.

"It's alright son, you don't need to say much. I missed you too," Rose said in comfort as she hugged me tighter.

From the door Djeny and Mikah came running in to give Rose a hug and say hello. They really liked my mom. They were excited as much as me because they rarely saw her. Even though my mom was not related to them they thought of her as a mother figure.

"Come into the living room sister" Tati said as she guided the way.

Hearing so I grabbed my mom's hand firmly and walked her to the living room. Tati pulled out a couple chairs and placed them in the middle of the room.

"Water or anything? You know what? Don't bother answering. Sit tight, I'll go grab you a cup of lemonade right now," Tati said as she headed for the kitchen.

Why is you hair so messy?" Rose asked me

" Sister was in the middle of braiding it then she stopped, I was waiting on somebody else to help me finish it." I responded.

"Okay pull out a chair and sit over here, where's the comb? and bring me some pomade."

"Okay okay i'll go get that right now"

I hurried into my bedroom and grabbed the comb I was recently using and sprinted back to the living room. By the time I got back, Tati and Rose were sharing a cup of lemonade and having a conversation. I knew better then too disturb adult conversation. Tati always said "adult talk is always important talk" So I walked into the kitchen and stared around the room wanting to past time.

"Now I see where you get such curly hair from" Djeny said as she creeped up on me.

"Your mom's a really beautiful lady and she looks really young too."

I stood quiet then responded as she was walking away."She really is right?"

About a minute went by and I was still staring into space, then Tati yelled out,"Batista bring your tiny butt over here. your mother don't got all day."

"coming!" I said As I rushed into the living room.

I got to the living room and Tati brought out a chair with her she borrowed from the kitchen. We had more seats in the living room but Tati really favored that chair more than the couch or the other seats in the room.

"Alright, I'll leave you two be. just callout if you need anything. our home is your home."

"Thank you cherie." Rose responded as she smiled at my aunt.

I took a chair and placed it down in front of Rose. It was a at good angle, that way her ams would have good space and she could braid my hair more flexible. There was a lot I wanted to talk to Rose about, so much I wanted to do, just to make up for lost time. I wanted to ask her if she had any plans for us to live together. It was rare to see her here so I wanted to ask her much more. Would she let me go back home with her? or if she planned on staying here with me. I wanted to spend the whole day with her. Maybe go out and take a walk, get some food at a restaurant. But I stayed quiet since no right words would come out. There was too much I wanted to say but I didn't know how to come out and say it. Finally she broke the awkward silence.

"Tomorrow is your sixth birthday am I right ?" Rose questioned me.

"It is isn't it? that thought wasn't going through my head, I could've went the whole day not realizing so."

"Haha that would've been a bummer, it's not every-day you get a sixth birthday."

"Yeah I guess so."I whispered.

My mother knew how I was feeling. I'm also sure she was feeling the same way. It's been two years now since I last seen her. And I remember it being for just a few days. The most memories I have of her is from pictures. And from my grandmother (Willot's mom) always telling me so much about her. She mentioned how my mother was a really smart lady. But her and my father met at a really young age. My mother was still in school. My dad already graduated and was a working man. And it was best for my dad to raise me, since they weren't together. My grand- mother told me not to ever have hard feelings towards my mother. "Just know that a mother will always do what's best for her child." Sure we missed out on a lot together, but i'm in her presence right now and that's what counts.

"You're going to church tomorrow assume?' Rose asked curiously.

"Yeah we are, we never miss a sunday."

"That's great to hear, make sure you pray for your mom here."

"Of Course I will." I said firmly.

"Now tell me about your girlfriend."

"Girlfriend.?" I asked shyly.

"Yes I know you have one by now."

"No I actually don't." I said nervously.

"You mean to tell me a handsome boy like you don't catch any girls eyes?"

" I guess not, or I just haven't noticed. Well there is this really cute girl at the church."

"Ooh church girl huh." Rose said teasingly.

"Yeah, she always dresses really nice, and the dress she always wears looks really nice . also her hair is really nice too, it's really curly and usually in a ponytail." I bragged on.

"Haha boy you're killing me. So that's the reason you

like going to church huh?"

"Not really but it could be half the reason." I said quietly.

"Well then at least you are honest."

"How long you plan on staying,?"

As much as I wanted her to answer. I knew I would heartbroken, knowing she would only be here for a short period of time.

"Ahh son you know I would spend all eternity here with you if I could. I live very far from here. I know it seems that life isn't fair and you're probably right, it isn't fair. You just have to be strong, you have lots of people here who loves you as much as I do. And they're in a much better position to take care of you then I am. It wouldn't be fair for me to give you less than you deserve. I just want what's best for you."

I sat silent for a moment, these weren't the words that I expected to hear from Rose, but it was the right words.

"I can already see it you being really important one day, you are going to change the world for the better. I can see that will burning inside of you."

I still sat there quietly, thinking to myself. What was it that I have that's so special. I mean i'm no different than any other 5 year old boy. How could I be so special? I sat and stared in space.

"But don't worry in time you to will see it. just know any of path you take is going to lead you to your destiny."

What my mother was saying made no type of sense to

me.

"You mean to say if I set my mind to going to the store, and I take a right turn instead of a left, i'll eventually get to the store."

I don't know why I even asked that question, if the store is on the left you obviously have to go left.

"No son here I can try to break it down for you so you understand."

"Yeah that'd be great." I said out loud.

"Say you want to be a professional fighter, and that's the path you're taking. You train everyday to become a great fighter then your fight date comes up. During the fight you get a devastating injury that took you out for the whole season. say your destiny was to be a writer, to write and connect with people. Instead of training, you started to write. You now discover that you love writing, it comes to you natural and easy. Since being a fighter wasn't destined for you, it jumped you in the path of writing which is your destiny."

Well this destiny thing makes a bit more sense. But how is it that a destiny is already written for you?, there should definitely be a way to cheat it. People can be anything they set their mind too not what their destined to be.

"What if I put all my heart and energy into being a fighter and I avoid writing totally.?'

I sat quiet waiting for Rose to respond.

"Well you can, but while doing so you might miss out on a lot that life had planned out for you. And later in life you might regret choosing the path you did. You should also do whatever your heart desires, don't be scared to take a chance, I have faith whatever path you walk on you'll do your best to perfect it."

What mother was trying to tell me were a lot to take in. I sat still and quiet for a couple minutes while she braided my hair. I thought of speaking out and gain some more knowledge but just being in her presence was enough for the moment.

"You finish that boys hair already?" Tati asked loudly as she made her way to the living room.

"Oh yeah, i'm about just done." Rose responded as she twisted my last braid.

"That boy sure is lucky to have your type of hair Come into the kitchen I have a plate of food waiting for you."

"Okay i'll be right there, you joining us son?" Rose reached out for my hand.

Not thinking twice I grabbed her hand then made our way to the dining table. It was just us three at the table. We shared laughs while we passed time. My aunt and my mom were mostly talking to each other While I sat and listened. To me this was the closest thing to a family dinner that I experienced in a while. It's usually me, my sisters, and my aunt who ate at the table, but Rose joined us today, she sat in the chair that's usually empty. that energy felt really good.

"Are you not going to eat son.?" Rose asked ready to share

her meal with me.

" No, he's ate plenty, if he eats another bite he'll start to cramp up. He learned his lesson from overeating. But don't worry I take care of this boy as if he was my own, i'll make sure he eats plenty so he grow big and strong. Right batis."

"Of Course that way i'll be able to take care of mom and she won't have to work so hard, and we'll be with each other everyday like a real family."

Tati stood quiet holding onto her lips as if she was going to tear up. Rose also sat quite while staring into my eyes. It's as if she was staring into my soul. I too was staring into her soul. It was hurt, her heart was hurt, it was lonely too, but her heart was strong. I had no idea you could tell so much by really looking into someone's eyes. Rose hugged me and I hugged her back while she cried. I too wanted to cry but I held everything in, I wanted to be her support and me crying would just make her sob more.

The room stood quiet, it was very sunny outside, you can see the rays going through the window making a rainbow on the floor. Rose seemed to have lost her appetite since she stopped eating and finished her lemonade.

" Hey how often does a bus show up out here anyway.?" Rose asked while taking a glimpse at the clock.

Tati took the dirty dishes from the table as she stood up to make her way to the sink.

"Ahh you know port-au-prince, so much movement going on, you never know what might happen. But if you leave here about 5:30 p.m, you'll soon get there at 5:50, if not sooner."

I quickly turned around and took a glimpse at the

clock hanging on the wall. It was ten minutes past five.

" ahh not fair why do you have to leave? Can't you just stay here, we definitely have enough room."

" I appreciate the offer son but this is your home not mine." Rose responded with a sad face.

"But Tati said our home is your home, isn't that so Tati.? It's just not fair you have to leave so soon."

"I know, but life isn't always fair to everyone, you'll always find advantages and disadvantages. Did we not have a great time today?"

" yes we did and I want it to be like that everyday." I said in tears.

Rose pulled me towards her and hugged me.

"Listen son remember what we talked about today, let it sink in. The will inside of you, let that be your push to achieve your goals."

" I guess it's time to say goodbye"

" you don't have to say goodbye, We are just separating ways for now. Map we ou talé.(I'll see you later)."

Rose hugged me one more time and kissed me on the forehead as she got ready to leave.

"Thanks a lot again for the food and for taking me in today."

"You're welcome, you are family and you're welcome here whenever you would like." Tati responded.

Rose grabbed her purse and headed for the door. She looked back once more and quickly turned away without waving. I guess she really doesn't like saying goodbyes. Now here I was standing in the same spot I was before when I was filled with curiosity. Now i'm filled with sadness and reality. I had to take in the truth that my mother was leaving. My heart felt good because I got too see her and I felt whole again in the moment . But I was also really sad she was leaving. And I didn't know the next time I would get too see her. I was asking myself a lot of questions. like why she just stay with me longer? But I'm pretty sure she already answered that. Right now I blame Nature she isn't always on my side. I had to be grateful for at least getting to see her and spending a bit of time with each other.

Tati was guiding rose downstairs to the exit door. I waited upstairs and stared out of the window. There I watched rose from her back as she walked away.

"Wow she braided your hair way better than I Did." Djeny said this with an amazed look on her face.

"Yes she did thanks for nothing.'I responded as I was walking away.

"Hey I was going to finish it up for you, I just needed to take a break, then you disappeared."

" well at least I got it done." I said with a tone.

"Next time you ask me to braid your nappy head, you better be paying me."

"With what money? The millions of dollars I make from work?."I said sarcastically.

Djeny walked and stood opposite to me and flicks my ear.

"You always gotta be smart huh? Just know next time

i'm charging you." she sticked out her tongue and made a funny face at me then ran into the other room.

"Stop all that talking I can barely hear the t.v." Mikah screamed and turned up the volume.

"Sorry" I whispered.

About a minute goes by Tati comes up walking into kitchen.

"Mikah close that TV you've been staring at that thing all day. Go take your brother a shower, and do the same for yourself after."

Almost everybody in my family had a short temper, plus you never knew when they would snap. Me and my sisters knew better than to argue with Tati. Mikah did as Tati said and closed the TV, but mumbled words to herself as she walked into the room.

"Batista come get your clothes!" Mikah yelled from the bedroom.

"Okay." I said nervously knowing she was frustrated at my aunt and me.

Whenever we'd need to take a shower, we went to the rooftop of the house. It was bigger than your average roof. We had chairs placed on top of the roof, and also tables. If you really wanted to you could have a small party up here. We used a pump to get our clean water. We used it for cooking, showering and drinking. To use the water, we would place a bucket underneath the tube and press the pump and water would flow down into the bucket.

I grabbed my clean clothes, towel, soap and headed to the roof. Mikah was up there waiting on me. She looked very impatient, so I hurried to her to not make her any more heated. I undressed once I got closer to her and place my clothes down and away so they would not get wet.

Once I got closer to mikah she dumped a bowl of water over my head to get my body wet. She grabbed the bar of soap and washed me all over. She then rinses me with the remaining water.It was always nice weather up here unless it was early mornings then you would freeze trying to shower. None of our neighbors could see us shower since we had a wall and our house was really tall.

"Here you're all set." Mikah said as she threw the towel over my head.

I took my time to dry myself off and get dressed. I took some deep inhales of the fresh air. It always felt good to breathe in the cool air after a bath. After I had gotten dressed I stood close to the edge of the roof. Up on the roof i could see a full view of the city, almost like a bird view. The city looked like a maze. I saw land for miles and houses for miles out to your eyes can see. It looked really beautiful. Our house was the tallest building around the area which made you see everyone's lives from up here. Some of my neighbors had really solid houses that stayed firm. Not everybody in my city or haiti could afford to own a house. some houses would be smaller and they would be cement walls and have strong rectangle plastic/medal ware as their rooftop for rain protection.

Coming up here at night time is the coolest thing you can do. The stars come out by the millions. you can see them so clear and close that you can count them yourselves. I sometimes wished that I could bring my bed up here to just sleep. But no matter how many stars up there that wish never came true.

"Hey make sure you don't fall kid you too close to the edge"

"Yeah i'll be carefull." I quickly responded to Mikah.

The wall was about three feet tall if not a little bit bigger. I was just barely reaching three feet close to four. The edge wasn't really my biggest worry, I knew I wouldn't fall. I obviously have the common sense. But i know Mikah was just being safe than sorry. Being so high up made me wonder if that's how it feels to run a nation, looking down on your followers and always have eyes over your people. The view had my eyes locked onto the city. I stared and stared until Mikah was done with her shower and we had to get going.

"Boy lets go before you fall to your death. And make sure you throw out the extra water." Mikah said this as she was putting her wet hair into a ponytail.

I don't get why she couldn't do it herself she used it last. I went on and emptied out the dirty water. We usually throw it down onto the soil, splashing on the ground getting anything near it wet. After we cleaned up the rooftop i made my way downstairs to the third floor.

"Awe look at you, tell me you don't feel better already." Tati asked with a smile.

I mean I did feel better, taking showers always made me feel better. Plus I just got my hair braided, so I did feel freshen up a little. I just didn't see the need to take a shower right at the moment. I said all this to myself then i responded.

"Yeah I feel better."

It was still really bright outside, I wanted to go out and play but that meant I had to get all sweaty again. I went into the kitchen and grabbed a piece of chicken, it's been a couple hours since I last ate now. Plus I got bored very easily in this house. Being around girl siblings everyday was a real drag. I sometimes wished I could trade one of my sisters for a brother, as awful as that sounds it was the truth. I wanted to play with somebody who had the same interest as me. Instead I was stuck with sisters, who all they did was braid hair or watch drama shows all day, and nag the hell out of me.

I sat in my room for a couple minutes. I laid down on my bed trying to fall asleep but that wasn't working. Finally I decided to join my sisters in the TV room, I joined them in watching their show. I stayed for about two episodes which was the longest hour and half of my life. It was now 9.00 p.m, really dark out. I asked Mikah if she wanted to go up to the rooftop and stargaze with me. Lucky me she agreed and we both went up to the roof. It was really quiet when we got up there, but the stars were everywhere to be seen, even though port-au-prince was the brightest city in Haiti, it was still really dark enough to see the stars. As a kid I had a really bright imagination, I started to name every star that I could count, I even named one after myself I would see it every time I went up to the roof. I counted its sister stars and compare it to my life.

I usually lay down on my back and look up. Once i started to look and pay close attention, all the stars that were invisible to me earlier finally showed up. Scattered everywhere, shining bright like the moon but hiding in plain sight. I know these stars are just one in a million, but since they made it here i wont do no complaining.

"You know we have to go back soon right."

"Yeah we could go in whenever you want to, these bugs are getting annoying anyway."

I smacked my face trying to kill a mosquito who was sucking on my blood. We fixed the sandals on our feet and headed for the stairs. Me and Mikah got to the room, Tati was sitting on Djeny's bed having a conversation.

"Finally you guys show up, quick let's sing a prayer and get you guys to bed."

We prayed for about a minute. I gave thanks to god for letting me see a new day, I give thanks for me having the chance to see my mother and a great day. I prayed for a new day. If I die before I wake, I pray my soul rest.

Since I shared a room with my sisters I sometimes get really annoyed. They would have convos all night and you can hear their voice echoing. Unless they added me to their conversation I didn't mind. The only positive outcome from sharing a room with my two sisters was the bedtime stories they would tell me. I favored scary bedtime stories a lot. Plus they knew more stories than anybody else I knew. Grandmother would tell them and they would tell me. So they don't get all the credit. I would sometimes get bunch of nightmares from scary stories, my mind was open to anything. To me anything was possible that's why I took these stories so literal. That was another reason sharing rooms wasn't the worst thing in the world, imagine being alone. All truth that saturday night was a quiet one. Besides the girlie conversations that echoed across the room. I tried my best to fall asleep which wasn't as hard. It's been a really long day and I sure needed the rest.

CHAPTER 2.

"April 5th"

"Ahh take that off right now!" Mikah shouted.

"I have it on already, this is what i'm wearing." Djeny responded.

"I don't care you know that's my favorite dress. Plus that's what I planned on on wearing today, you could've at least asked me first."

"You probably would've said no anyways so why bother."

Still laying in bed I grabbed my pillow and covered my head trying to avoid the conflict of my two annoying sisters. It was about everyday that they would fight over clothes, food, hair nots, or t.v shows. Lucky enough I learned how to ignore them.

"You girls need to stop all that noise, it's too early for me to be getting a headache. Djeny take off your sister's dress, and find something else to wear." Tati said as she made her way into our room.

"But I don't have any other outfits to wear, and she wore this last time." Djeny sat on her bed puts on a really sad face and began to argue her point once more.

" it's not fair, it's because she's older, she always gets whatever she wants."

" girl stop, i'm well sure I bought you more than enough dresses, four to be exact. That's one for every sunday of the month."Tati said with a serious tone."And start to wake up your brother, he still needs to get cleaned up." Tati walked out and closed the door.

I was wide awake on my bed trying, to get a couple more minutes of sleep. But that was impossible with this much chatter going on in the morning. About a minute later Mikah yelled from the top of her lungs as if she was trying to wake me up from the dead.

"Batista get up!."

Her voice shoved me off my bed landing on the floor. I stood up standing opposite of her with a mean mug on my face.

"What!? I'm not dead you know." I said sarcastically.

"Yeah it sure looked like you were to me." Mikah said teasingly. "But since you're up, come up to the rooftop, Tati got your clothes ready. And make sure you do your bed." Mikah demanded, then closed the door.

I took a deep breath and fell backwards on my bed. I knew I had to get ready soon, church started at eight A.M and it was about ten past seven. Being late to church in my neighborhood was like a sin. The other churchmates would gossip around to the other peoples about you when you walk into the church late. They would give you dirty looks as if you just committed a crime. The most famous insult was the stare. They would roll their eyes at you and make a "chirp" noise with their mouth. That was called the silent insult. But we never had to witness that ourselves, since Tati always brought us a on time or a couple minutes early.

"Boom!" the door opened.

"Seriously dude you're taking a nap and you have me wait-

Laurent Joseph

ing on you."

" sorry Mikah i'm just tired."

"You know you can shower yourself."

But I ignored her comment and made my way up to the roof. There Djeny was also bathing herself, and Tati was hanging some clothes that she had just wash.

"Bonjour Tati." I said with a smile.

"Hi batis, c'mon get ready fast we don't wanna be late."

It was a really cold morning, plus the water Mikah splashed me with was usually cold. Once she threw the water at me I was wide awake, she then soaped me all over then rinsed me once more. Afterward Mikah would throw me a towel to wrap around with.

I went downstairs to get dress. Tati already had an outfit picked out for me. Unlike my sisters I didn't take forever to get ready, I quickly got dressed and went to the kitchen where Tati had cooked some breakfast for us. By the time I finished my meal everybody was ready to head out. Mikah and Djeny quickly grabbed a piece of food, and headed for the door. It was about a fifteen minute drive to the church. If we left right now we could make it right on time. The car ride to church is mostly loud because of my 2 sisters, and sometimes we would all share laughs. But today was not so loud, it was an awkward silence all the way there.

Taking a ride through the city was full of life. But also had its down parts. Seeing my people struggle was really sad. On the side of the roads tables were set up. Mother's would have baskets on top of their head. Which would carry fruits, vegetables, and water bags. And if you were a guy you would be selling other supplies. Usually they would have things made from scratch like sandals, shoes that were made from recycled tires. Sometimes guys would also sell food or clothes, or cooking materials. In haiti a lot of people are merchants. Most people would have a skill there good at. Say cooking. They would make the best food possible and have some varieties. Then you'd need a food stance and a busy corner to post up so you can have more commerce. Everyday families will do this. This is how they pay for their kids education, daily needs, and just plain out for survival.

We arrived at the church five minutes after eight, which meant we were late. Walking in I seen about two older woman looking over and rolling their eyes at us. I ignored it and went on about my business. The pastor had already started preaching. We found a seat in the back of the aisle and decided to sit there. I quickly caught up with what the pastor was preaching about. "What it means to have faith." what the pastor preached. Not everything he was saying made sense to me. I would start to listen for a couple minutes then I would fall asleep. Tati woke me up and told me to go join the kids section. I never liked going to the kids section, but it was way less boring than the adult section.

I went down to the basement where the bible study took place. Down here they also had the kitchen room. A big open space you can open up tables, and place out chairs to eat after the service was over. I got to the bible study late because I took my time to get there. I hurried to the circle, pulled out a chair and took a seat. I sat right across from Bella. She's the girl I looked forward to seeing whenever I get to church. She was really nice. Me and her talked sometimes but just as friends nothing more. Everybody had a book expect for me. I came late and forgot my book. what else could go wrong. Before our teacher had a chance to ask me about why I don't have out my book, Bella quickly raised her hand and shouts.

" i'll share my book with him."

Bella grabbed her chair, lifted it up 5 inches off the ground, moved towards me and sat right beside me. I blushed a bit of the fact she was sitting so close to me.

"Wow your hairs almost longer than mine." bella said with an amazed face as she pulled out the end of my ponytail.

"Hands to yourself." the teacher yelled from across the circle.

We both stayed quiet for no more than ten seconds. Bella started to tease the teachers about her glasses. On how they were so close to falling. It was resting at the edge of her nose, it looked pretty funny.

'haha.' we both shout out with laughter.

"You two can join your parents upstairs if that's how you want to behave in my class."

The teacher said this with a really serious face. That face meant stop the nonsense or leave. We both thought it was best if we left. But instead of going back to adult section we walked around the church for a bit. We found corner where all the adults couldn't see us. We stayed quiet then I said something wanting to make conversation.

"Hey how much time till church ends anyway.?"

"Just about one more hour." bella responded.

"So what do you plan on doing until that time.?" I asked.

"I don't care, whatever you wanna do."

But I didn't know what to do, it was the first time I was alone with a girl that wasn't my sister. I stay quiet not

knowing what to say.

"First we need to make sure we don't get seen by adults." bella said this while grabbing my wrist and moving closer to me. She leaned in and kissed me on the lips for about five seconds. She leaned back, smiled and tells me.

"Happy birthday."

"How did you know it was my birthday.?"

"Remember you told me of the date a couple sundays ago."

"Yeah I do remember, it's just me, myself barely can remember my own birthday, i'm surprised you didn't forget."

"Of Course not silly it's not everyday you get a birthday."

I smiled and she smiled back, I stared in her eyes. Her eyes were the clearest shade of brown. Plus her skin tone made her eyes glow out even more.

"Your eyes are so beautiful." I mumbled to myself.

"What's that.?" bella asked.

"You're pretty, I mean your eyes they're pretty."

"Thank you,you really think so." bella said while

blushing.

For so long I had a crush on her but I never had the courage to step up and admit it. Now here we are, she was the first person to tell me happy birthday, and she also give me my first birthday gift which was my first kiss. We stared at each other for a really long time but the vibe didn't change.

"You think we should go back to the adults now, we've been gone a pretty long time."

"Yeah we probably should do that, what will our excuse be?" I asked nervously.

"Not sure but i'm going back now, see you later."

"Bye."

I said this as she walked away in through the double doors. I was feeling kind of sad, knowing I would have to wait until next sunday to see her again. I stood around for a couple minutes until she had gone in so I could follow. I did this just so it wouldn't look as if we were together. I go into the adult section and took a seat next to Tati. Before she got a chance to ask where i've been the pastor told everybody to stand up for the final prayer. It felt as if the pastors prayer went on forever. We sung a chorus with the church then prayed. The church service ended and we went on on home. Tati never enjoyed staying after the service to eat or hang out. She mostly didn't enjoy the church food because she says she's witness mice running around the kitchen. After hearing that I almost puked and was ready to head on out. I wanted to stay for one reason and it was to hang out more with bella, but i'm pretty sure she already went home.

On the way back Tati made a quick stop by this lady who were selling fruit. She picked out four mangos one for each of us, including cooking matter like carrots, and some other vegetables. I love mangos, me personally think it's the best fruit. It has a lot of sugar and you can eat about a thousand of them and you would feel fine. If anybody was stuck on getting me a birthday gift just think of mangos. I'll gladly take it. When we arrived to the house as soon as we parked, I ran upstairs rushing to my room to get undress. I took off my church clothes and laid down on my bed with a huge blush on my face.

"What got you so hyper and giggly boy." Tati asked as she made her way into my room. "And don't think I didn't see you earlier with Jacques daughter, you kids think you're so slick."

"Oh you knew huh.?"

"Of Course but don't worry about it, it's natural for a boy to like a girl. Your mother and father liked each other that's how you were born. Just be careful I don't wanna see a mini you walking around this house just yet." Tati said with a smile "And your father wanted to speak to you, he should be waiting on you right about now."

"Okay i'll go down in a second."

I procrastinated for a really long time and stayed laying on my bed, I was really exhausted from church. It's about half an hour past noon. Tati is halfway through getting dinner ready. My sisters are in the living room as usual watching drama shows. You could say me and casper the friendly ghost had a pretty strong bond, since I was always talking and hanging out with myself. I recalled that my dad wanted to see me. I should probably go see what he wants.

Just as I was having that thought Tati yelled out from the kitchen.

"Ahh!!"

I ran to the kitchen to see what the commotion was about.

"It's a rat big ones too, about two of them, came running from out the tube right there."

Tati pointed out the long tube that she witnessed the rats came out from.

"I'm too old to be moving like that, one wrong fall and your poor auntie right here gonna break her back."

I stood around not knowing what to do. My sisters joined the show just a second later. I seen Djeny with a broom in her hands. But what was she planning on doing with it. Try to sweep it? or maybe hit it away. But that would only make it even more pist off. I don't see why that was an option. I feel like everybody should just relax for a minute and take a deep breath. They should worry about setting traps or something, am I really the only with a brain here. As much as I don't want rats around the house, I much rather want food scavenger rats, not mean angry rats, coming back for revenge because we just tried beating it with a broom. Or maybe i'm just thinking about this situation too deep. Maybe they could actually kill it with a broom, but either way I didn't want to be a part of it.

"Hey watch out." I said this to djeny as i made my way to the door.

"Where you think you're going boy, so now there's a rat you want to leave." Tati said

"You guys can handle it it's just two rats and there are three of you." "Alright boy go see your dad, he's been waiting on you for the past hour now."

My sister moved to the other side clearing the way as if they were waiting on an approval. I avoided them and headed for the door that leads to the stairs.

"Hey dad Tati said u wanted to talk to me."

"Yes son come on in." willot said as he turned off his phone.

I slowly walked into the kitchen. His part of the house was more neat than the floor we lived on. But ours was bigger. It's because he had it all to himself so that makes sense.

"You're getting tall kid." willott said as he made his way towards me.

"Yeah that's what comes with aging."

"Yeah that's why I called you down here, I wanted to give you something."

Willot pulled out a stack of money from his pockets and thumbed through it, in my mind I was thinking about why he had so much cash. Only pulling out the smallest bills he hands out to me twenty dollars.

" ahh man this is a lot of money." I screamed out with excitement.

"Yeah make sure you put it to good use, i've been waiting on you all day, don't your aunt tell you not to have adults wait on you."

"Yeah you're right,but today's been a long day."

"Yeah it has been, but I have to head out right now, tell your aunt to save me a couple plates of the food if she's cooking."

"Yeah definitely will do."

"Alright i'll see you later then."

I had to walk out with him just so he could lock his doors. After he went down to the first floor and headed for his car i went back up to the third floor.

"That was fast are you sure you seen your father." Tati asked as I made my way into the kitchen.

"Yes he was just in a rush."

"That damn fool, never has time to settle down and spend time with his kids."

I avoided Tati's comment and went into my room to put away the money I just got. My sisters were still in the living room watching T.V. Tati was preparing a big meal maybe she was doing this because of my birthday but i'm not too sure yet. I had a shoe box with the wrapping paper still inside of it. I decided that's where I wanted to hide my money.

"Where you get all that money from." Djeny asked as she ran towards me.

"Don't worry about it you noisey." I responded.

"Calm down i'm just curious."

"Dad gave it to me for my birthday present."

"Oh cool so now you can pay me to do your hair."

"Yeah okay like that's going to happen."

"Okay be like that, all those favors I did for you and I can't get a dollar."

"Okay, whatever here just leave me alone."

'cool, alright happy birthday big head."

Djeny left the room and I sprinted back to the shoe box as fast as possible. I really did not mind giving her a dollar, she just really aggravates me when she's noisy and she wont stop till she gets what she wants. I hope my next birthday present is a 6 year old brother. But sure like that'll ever happen.

I should probably go outside now since there isn't much else to do in here. There were two other people I enjoyed playing with and they were both my neighbors. Our house was on a dead end street and both of their houses were opposite from mine. There were about five houses on our street and everybody knew each other, I could go all the way down the street but I wasn't allowed to leave or I would get a whooping once I got back.

There was a lot of different punishments you can get. It all depends on what you did. The worst punishments was you had to stay on your knees and hold up a block or a bible in your palms. If you happen to drop the blocks or the bible you would need to start your time over. I seen that happen to my neighbor friends a couple of times but never happened to me.

I heard a soccer ball being kicked around, I decided to go take a peek and see who it was. It ended up being rudy. Rudy was my pal, he was my neighbor and he was also the same age as me. I was excited to tell him about what happened at church but he probably wouldn't believe me anyway. I needed somebody to go outside with me. I went up to Djeny in the living room.

"Hey Djeny since I gave u money can u take me outside?"

"Sure why not, it's really sunny outside right now" Djeny took of her sweatshirt leaving only her short sleeve cause of the heat outside.

I quickly went and changed into some more comfortable clothes, Djeny was waiting for me by the door.

"Hey hurry up" she yelled as I rushed to her.

Djeny was always the impatient type so I hurried to her and we raced downstairs to the door. I opened up the door and rudy was outside kicking the ball against the wall. I rushed to him to go say what's up.

"Hey Rudy." I called out to him.

"Hey Batis, whatchu up to.? Rudy responded.

"nothing, how come you didn't' tell me you were outside I would've came out earlier with you if I knew." i said.

"Ehh I thought you were busy, plus I didn't know you came back from church already."

"Yeah the service ended a little bit early today, you won't believe what happened today."

"I probably won't but go head tell me."

"Remember that girl Bella I kept telling you about?"

"How could I not remember that's all you talk about."

"Well she kissed me today."

"Really? I mean I guess that's hard to believe but it could be true, good for you kid."

Rudy was the same age as me but his height outmatched mine so he looked a bit older. Just because of that he thought he could keep calling me kid, we're both kids he shouldn't be kidding me. But I didn't mention that to him.

"Yeah it was pretty awesome." I responded while laughing.

Rudy and I started to kick the ball to each other back and forth.

"Hey did you bring out your marbles?' Rudy asked.

"Of Course I did, is that really a question."

"Just wondering cause i've been out here for a while now and i'm getting pretty tired this heat is killing me."

"Yeah, if you set up a couple holes we can get a game started."

"Yeah sure let's get that done right now."

Knock off marbles was one of my favorite games to play. I was so good that I would compete at school against anybody who thought they were better. The game worked like this. You can have how ever much players you want. Say two players are playing. you make a hole and you're supposed to shoot your marble so that it hits your opponent's marble and make it go inside the hole. But your mable is to stay outside the hole, then you can keep shooting and try to knock off other opponents.

Me and Rudy played and competed against each other a lot. We only played to see who was better, whoever won got to keep their marbles. But if it were a random person we didn't know, we would play to keep their marbles. I had the confidence to play for keeps, so a lot of times I played and kept the marbles I won.

"Hey batista hurry up here dinner is ready." Mikah yelled from the window while staring down at us.

"Hey is that your sister up there." Rudy asked pointing up at the house.

"Yeah it is, I don't know why she's buggin me, we haven't been out here for that long." I said while still trying to knock his marble into the hole.

"I'm actually going in pretty soon, so if you would to go in right now we could come back out after you eat dinner."

"Awe man you're just scared i'm winning, so you're avoiding me."

"Yeah like you'll ever beat me, but hey you can keep this as a birthday present."

Rudy pulled out two marbles from his pockets. The marbles he gave me were one of the most clear and beautiful crystals i've ever seen, I don't get why he was giving them to me. These marbles were really rare to find so I was resistant into taking them.

"You sure you want to give them to me.?" I asked.

"Yeah why not, next time we play i'll win them back anyway." rudy laughed in a teasing way.

"Okay let's see if that happens."

I took the marbles and stared at them as if I just got gold. I knocked off the last marble he had on the floor with the one he just gave me, then placed them into my pocket.

"Hey I should get going I actually need to go take a shower right about now."

"Okay I needa hurry to Mikah before she jumps out the window to come get me." we both laughed out loud and dapped up as we went our separate ways.

Djeny was still sitting on the front stairs waiting for me, but she looked really patient. The whole time I was out there she didn't bother me at all which surprised me. But I wasn't complaining, I snapped my fingers in her face to bring her back to reality, since she was gazing out into space.

"Hey you done already?" Djeny asked as as she jumped up.

"Yeah we could go up now, i'm all set."

"You smell that? That's the food Tati is cooking for your birthday." Djeny said while taking in a deep breath.

"Yeah before I went outside I noticed she was cooking, i'm ready to eat up."

"Then let's hurry up before Mikah eats everything."

"Yeah let's go."

We both rushed up, racing through the stairs. We got up to the living room Mikah wasn't there surprisingly. Djeny shoved me from the couch and grabbed the remote controller switching the channel to some show. I shook my head and walked out. I wasn't feeling like watching what she had on. I walked into the kitchen and Tati had the table set up with a feast. There was a really big bowl of fried chicken, then another bowl with cooked rice and beans, she also had potato salad, and a bunch of other delicious looking food. My mouth started to water a ton by just glimpsing at the table view.

"Hey kid, don't think you're going to eat without washing up first." Tati said as she placed more food onto the table.

"Yeah i'll make sure I clean up first."

I go into the bathroom washing my hands and washing off the dirt that was stained on my marbles. I left the bathroom to go into my room, Mikah was sitting on her bed, it looked as if she was reading because of the book that she had in her hand. I didn't want to bother her but she needed to go take me a shower.

"Hey Mikah can you take me a shower?" I asked nervously.

She looked at me then looked away ignoring me for a minute. I went to my bed to put away all my marbles.

"You're a big boy now you can shower yourself, you know the process, it's not like you're learning how to do magic or something."

I guess she was right, I knew how to get myself clean, I was just scared I would get soap into my eyes. But it couldn't be that bad, I guess i'll give it a try. I still needed somebody to be up there with me, Tati would never let me go up there by myself. I knew Mikah would get annoyed if I asked her to bring me up to the rooftop, but I was hungry and I needed to shower and eat.

"Hey Mikah i'll shower myself but I still need somebody to go up there with me." a long pause went by and she didn't respond.

"So do you want to bring me up?" I asked.

"Okay kid whatever makes you happy, give me a

minute"

"Okay take your time.. it's not like i'm hungry or anything." I said sarcastically.

"Okay let's go."

Mikah grabbed her book she was reading and we went up to the roof. It was pretty warm outside so I didn't mind the water being a little bit cold. I grabbed the bucket and placed it under the pump and filled it up almost to the top. I rinse myself with a bowl of water, then I applied soap on my body and rinsed myself.

"That wasn't that bad," I thought to myself.

I had brought my clothes with me. I placed them down somewhere they wouldn't get wet. I grabbed my towel to dry myself, then I got dressed. Tati had told me to wear something nice for the diner so I picked out a nice shirt and some nice shorts. I didn't want to try too hard. Mikah was sitting on the wall of the roof and didn't seem in a hurry so I myself didn't hurry.

"Hey what are you reading?' I asked with curiosity, it was the first time is seen her read.

"Something that's not your age material." Mikah responded with an attitude.

I really didn't see the need for an attitude I was just asking a question, I don't get why everybody in my family has an attitude. I'm really starting to see that it's not healthy.

"Okay well we can go back now, i'm all set" I said with a tone.

"Okay."

We both headed downstairs to the kitchen, Djeny was still out in the living room. Tati was about done with dinner and she was taking a rest, sitting back on her chair.

"Awe look at you all dressed up."

I really wasn't dressed up, I just had on a nice shirt with some khaki shorts. But I went along with it, it was nice to get a compliment I guess. Tati got up and went into her room and grabbed her towel and some clean clothes. I'm pretty sure she was going to shower. For about 15 minutes all I was doing were sitting around with Mikah watching her read her book. Tati came down and she had a nice blue dress on and her hair done. To me she was the one who deserved a compliment not me.

"Hey you two go and get yourself ready were having dinner soon." Tati said.

"And batista you can go invite your friend rudy over if you want to."

I was pretty excited to go and call him over for dinner, I knew he would want to anyway. I was already prepared just waiting on everybody else. I went on outside and hurried to rudy's house. I got to his door and hit on the door a couple times. A minute later Rudy's mom came out and opened the door. She was a beautiful lady with really long hair that shine when the sun hit on to it.

"Hey kid what's up." she said while smiling at me knowing I wasn't here to chat with her probably looking for Rudy.

"Hi, Tati told me to ask Rudy if he wanted to join us for dinner today since it's my birthday."

Haitian people weren't always okay with their kids going to eat at other people's houses just because of their pride. They think they would get judge and other people would think they are poor and cannot feed their children. But me and rudy had been living close to each other for a while now and Tati and my dad had been friends with his parents for a pretty long time so I don't see why he couldn't join us.

"I don't see why not, we were just about to have dinner ourselves but I don't see why not." she stood still staring at me then called out to Rudy.

"Rudy, your friend is here to bring you to dinner."

No more than a second went by and Rudy came running towards the door, he too was dressed up and ready to go.

"Yeah sure let's go." he said with excitement.

"Okay behave yourself over there boy." his mother said with a strict voice.

We both left I waved goodbye to his mother. we went on across the street where my house was. Rudy also had a pretty nice house. Instead of it being tall and big. it was shorter and it was wider but it looked really nice from the outside and in the inside. We got to the dining room and everybody was sitting at the table with hungry eyes on their face, ready to eat up the table.

"Hey we better hurry up before they eat us instead of the food."

I sat next to Rudy at the table. Djeny and Mikah sat opposite from us and Tati sat at the beginning of the table.

"Ahh man today was a long day, let's say a prayer and get to eating already."

We all stared at Tati waiting on directions for what we were to do. We were told to grab each other hands and form a circle around the table and we sung a prayer over the food we were about to eat. We prayed for no more than a minute, Tati give thanks for me seeing another birthday, for the fact we had the gift of having so much food to eat and for other days to come. This dinner was a long and filled with laughter. I had a lot of other dinners and birthdays but everything that happened on that day and the day before got stuck to my memory and that'll be the days I never forget.

After we were finished eating me and rudy went up to the roof. Since I was older now I was able to go up by myself. The sun was starting to set and the sky was looking really red. That is another reason why I like the color red. Seeing that color in the sky is one of the best views I ever saw, plus I seen it with my best friend. We both gazed at the stunning sky and thought of the future and how many more times we'll get to see the sky like this. From that day we both picked red as our favorite color.

Mikah came up to the roof about 30 minutes later joining us. She also had brought up the book she was reading. She told me it was about how to not get annoyed having a younger brother who has a lot of needs. I was kinda shocked. Yes I had a lot of needs but that's only because I was young and Tati didn't want me to do anything on my own. I was feeling better that she told me what the book was about since I was really curious.

"Hey Rudy your mother was expecting you back

soon, she told me to give you a heads up."

We both felt aggravated, we were just starting to have fun. Me and rudy didn't go to the same school, so I only seen him mostly in the weekends or after school when he's home. Me and Mikah started to walk rudy to his house, we got outside and Rudy pulled out his marbles and said.

"Hey you want to get one more game of knock off before we have to go inside." Rudy asked.

"Ahh man you think we'll have time?" I asked knowing Tati would be calling up for me soon.

"I mean staying out here for a couple more minutes won't hurt, the sun hasn't went down fully yet."

I pulled out the marbles that I always carried in my pockets and set them on the floor. Rudy had his marbles out, he set his pieces on the floor and was ready to attack my set piece. we both played until the sun set over our heads, then we went our separate ways.

CHAPTER 3.

"Back to school."

Getting up for school wasn't so bad. I usually had to drag myself out of bed to get ready. Mikah and Djeny were always up before me. Since the school we attended made us wear uniform, I didn't have to hear my sisters crying about what they would wear all the time. We all went to the same catholic french school. They let you speak only in french and not haitian-creole. Over at the school speaking haitian-creole was like a sin. It was improper and it was not the language of the school. Since at home everybody spoke haitian-creole, I would sometimes mix french and haitian-creole in my sentences, and my teachers did not like that one bit.

"Batista get your but up, you're always the one last to be ready." Mikah said with a high tone voice.

"Why are you guys so energetic in the morning anyway." I asked as I yawned, crawling out of my bed.

"You like sleep too much, didn't grandma tell you that sleep is the cousin of death."

I recall my grandma saying something like that. But that didn't help the fact that I was tired. My sisters are always trying to find a way to kill something that I enjoyed. Sleep was one of those things.

"boy were leaving soon go and take a shower, you're a big boy now you can get yourself ready." Mikah said as she left the room.

I was happy that I was older but it seemed that just being one year older came with a lot more responsibilities. Tati had already picked out my uniform, it was a navy blue shirt, with black pants or sometimes I would wear khaki shorts. I didn't mind wearing the uniform. It made me look a bit professional. My sisters had to wear a dress with an undershirt. They also looked professional, but more like school girls.

Every morning before we headed for school, Tati would pack us our lunch for the day. That was my favorite part of school, getting to eat the food Tati had made. She would make us fried plantains, not the regular ones but the sweet kind. which made my mouth water just thinking of it. With some fried chicken, sweet potatoes, and a bunch of other goodies into our lunchbox. Me and my sisters were thankful for that because we ate plenty when it was lunch-time at school.

I had showered and got dressed. I started to eat breakfast and waited on my sisters to come, so we could start walking to school. Our school was about 35 minutes away. In the morning there were always a bunch of commotion. The center of port-au-prince was filled with life. A bunch of other kids were making there way to school, people going to work and so much more. On the side streets you would sometimes see street performers. They would do a bunch of cool things. Some would be singing, doing tricks, and such. My favorite trick I saw was a guy who took a stick that was in flame and placed it into his mouth. After he took it out his mouth the flame was gone, then he smacked both his cheeks and blew out a gigantic flame. That was the coolest thing i've ever seen up close. Till this day I ask myself how he did it, But i know magicians rarely share their secrets.

Since there were a bunch of commotion in the mornings. The streets had a lot of frantic activity. That meant violence would sometimes occur and you would see more cops than usual. Around that time kidnapping rates were really high. This mostly occurred in the mornings when a bunch of kids are making their way to school or coming back from school. A kid from a school nearby got kidnaped one time and they asked his parents for money, way more money they could get their hands on. Since those kidnappers were heartless and did not get what they wanted, they reacted cowardly and violently. A couple weeks later they had found the kid's body near his school with a bag over his head. Since then my dad and aunt made sure we were really careful. A lot of cops started to patrol the mornings and after school activities. But kidpanings were not a rare thing at that time around these parts of haiti, packed with a lot of people. My dad was into politics and getting rid of those type of criminals so he had a lot of enemies. People were always sending him threats about attacking him wear it hurts, which were his kids. since they couldn't get to him personally.

Me and my sisters only had to take one bus to get to our school. After a while Tati stopped going with us when the temperature on the streets went down, and we started going by ourselves again. It was a risk. But that's for everything in life. She didn't want us to be scared of where were from, so we made our way to school the three of us everyday. I wasn't really scared going to school I had trust in my sisters that they would keep me safe. The people around me also weren't bad people, if they seen something happening to us they would reach out to help. Everywhere you go there will be bad people and good people. Once you find the balance its almost magical.

That morning we arrived at the school just a couple minutes late. Since we weren't with our parents we had to find a way to sneak in. there was a big gate in front of the school that you had to go through. All the students waited out front until 8:15 am for it to open up until 8:25 the gate closed. If you were late you would have to ring the bell with your parents with you. Me and my sisters knew that wasn't a option at the moment. We made our way around the school. There was a fence and under it was a hole that's used as a drain, where water would go down if it rained. Thankfully it was dry that day. Djeny went first then we give her our bookbag and I made my way then Mikah made her way in.

The school was an elementary and middle school Djeny and mikah were both in middle school and I was in second grade. So we all had to go our separate ways. The school was on a really big campus, it took me a couple minutes to get to my class. I passed all the older kids on the campus who were making their way to class. Luck wasn't on my side that day. Just a minute away from my class I seen a teacher, she called me up asking why I wasn't at class.

"Hey kid where you supposed to be, you're definitely not a 8th grader, elementary classes are that way. And if you're late where's your pass."

"I actually don't have a pass miss." I responded nervously.

"So you're telling me you snuck in."

"Yeah but only." I tried to finish my sentence but she

cut me off.

" No butts child you come with me."

I knew I was in for trouble, going to the principal's office this early in the morning. A lot of kids get caught sneaking into school. That was the worst thing to do here and the punishment wasn't pretty. I knew I had to make up an excuse so I wouldn't have to deal with the principle. If I told them I was late because I was watching street performers I would get a punishment. But it'd still get one either way for sneaking in. I could say the streets were really busy and they really were and I wouldn't be lying.

I got to the principal's office and the were a couple other kids in there. His first reaction of me was a funny look. it was the first time I was getting in trouble by him. Other times it was just by my teachers. He was a really scary looking dude. I tried my best to remain calm and waited on him to see what he would do with me. The teacher who brought me to his office whispered in his ear about the situation he looked at me and shook his head.

"Is that right.?" he said out loud.

I stayed quiet not really knowing what to say. I didn't want to annoy him by saying the wrong thing.

"Well at least he was making his way to class. He should get some credit for that, as long as this isn't an everyday thing he's all set to go back."

"whow ' I whispered to myself, I can't believe I wasn't going to get in trouble. That was a first.

"You're all set to go back kid, class should be starting very soon, can you make your way over there, or do you need to be accompanied.?'

46

"I'm all set I remember where my class is." I responded quickly.

"Okay make your way over there."

"yes sir, thanks a lot."

I quickly got up, left his office, and made my way out the door. I'm glad I wasn't with my sisters, all of us together would've probably made it worse. The elementary classes was all the way in the back of the campus. It was about a 5 minute walk to get to there. Before I got inside I saw a couple kids skipping. They were in the back of the church playing marbles. I was really taunted to go join them but I just got lucky, and my luck wouldn't be the same if I would to get caught again. I ignored them and made my way into class.

"Hey look who's joining us." my teacher shouted as I made my way into the class. I had a couple friends in my class, they were all good people. All the boys sat in the middle row of the class, the girls sat in the front, nobody sat in the back row. Today's class looked pretty small maybe it's because of the commotion going on the city this morning.

'Hey Joseph." John called out to to me as I placed my bookbag on the floor.

'Sa kap fet john." I hollered back.

"Hey you just got here no chit chat, today were doing addition so you best pay attention." my teacher said to me and john.

I stayed quiet and faced forward at the board. Two plus five, and a bunch of other problems was what we were learning. Math was not my favorite subject. I really did know what to do, I just never liked dealing with numbers too much. Seeing a lot of numbers on the board and doing equations give me a headache.

"Okay Joseph what's eight plus eight." my teacher pointed to me.

"Mwen pa konnen.' which means "i don't know." but I said this in creole and I was supposed to say . "je ne sais pas" which is french.

"What did you say?" the teacher asked.

"I don't know" I said again but this time I fixed my mistake and repeated it in french. "Je ne sais pas"

"That's what I thought, this is a french school and we speak french in here not creole at home you speak creole not here."

I really didn't see why we couldn't speak in creole. It's basically the same language as french just twisted up a bit. It's not like you don't understand what i'm saying. But I kept that thought in my head. if I had spoken out I would have gotten hit by the ruler. Especially with my teachers really short patience. School was almost over for the year there was a week and a half left until summer came about. I just needed to bang out these couple days until I could relax. There was this girl who sat right beside me. we always made conversation whenever we got the chance too. If i'll miss anybody she'd be the one I miss the most.

About an hour of listening to the teacher, and doing handouts recess had come about. It was time to go outside and take a rest from all this work. We had about 45 minutes for recess, there was a lot to do, all of these kids had a bunch of energy. Everybody was quick to leave the classroom. Me and farah stayed back and decided to walk out together.

"Hey what made you late this morning?" Farah asked as we made our way out of the classroom.

"Uhh today was a really busy day, there was a bunch of traffic, plus this performer was doing a bunch of cool tricks so we decided to watch him for a couple minutes."

"Oh I see, did you have to sneak in under the fence.?" she asked

"Yeah but I got caught halfway, my sisters were fine tho."

"Did you have to go see the principle?"

"Yeah but he give me a pass surprisingly."

"Oh that's cool, it's not like him to give kids a pass, maybe it's because it's your first time or schools almost over so he has a good spirit this month."

"Mhm who knows i'm just glad I didn't get in trouble."

"Yeah me too." Farah smiled and we both ran to the court-yard where everybody else was playing at. We usually gathered around and played soccer. The older kids were on the field away from us. We stayed at the courtyard. We didn't always get the chance to use a soccer ball so we used whatever we could get. Usually we would use an empty water bottle, or any type of bottle, then set up a goal with 2 rocks on each side as the goal. It was a cheap way to play but it worked for us and we weren't complaining. I was pretty skilled at soccer so whenever there was a game about to happen everybody would want me to be on their team.

"Hey joseph come play." John shouted across the yard.

"Ahh i'm not really feeling like sweating right now, maybe at lunch."

that was the first time I said no to playing soccer. I was trying to vibe with my friend farah and playing soccer wasn't going to help. The girls usually watch us play soccer. Or they would be taking turns playing jump ropes and a bunch of other girly activities. They were pretty skilled at it too. But we both stayed on the sideline watching everybody else play as we enjoyed our conversation. Farah didn't live close to me and school was the only place I got too see her at, so I would miss her the whole summer.

"Hey wanna go walk around the hill."

"Sure if we have time." Farah responded.

On the same hill where our classes were, there were vacant buildings/old classrooms that weren't being used. We heard stories about what happened here. The most famous story was about this girl who died around one of the classrooms. Her name was Elizabeth. She supposedly haunts the classrooms around the hill. If you went there alone you would be really scared. Since we were all young we believed in the horror and never went alone.

"Actually I think I might play a quick game of soccer, we got a little bit of time left." i said to farah.
"Yeah go ahead." she responded

"Hey john let me join in is that cool." I asked.

"Well you could've when we had an open spot, but you can watch now."
"Ahh man alright."

"Next game you can join." John said firmly.

I guess that's my fault. I could've joined in earlier, but now I want to play and can't, that's really annoying. Me and Farah stayed on the bleachers and watched the other kids play. She kept staring at the girls who were jump roping, it was a strong sign that she wanted to join them, but I think she enjoyed my company a bit more. We hung out for a couple more minutes then the bell rung for us to go back to class.

"What a drag." I thought to myself

"Hey we got lunch really soon tho so don't stress it." Farah said to me.

"Yeah you're right."

We got back to class and the teacher had a sheet on our desk with a book that had cursive writings. Our task was to copy the words from the book down onto the sheet word for word. I didn't mind writing at all that was the easiest thing we could do in this class. We had to write until lunch time came about.

"Turn your papers into me when you are done." the teacher announced to the class.

"All done." Farah shouted! making her way to the front of the room. I was also done so I too went to turn my paper in.

"Great job class, that wasn't bad right." the teacher said with a smile on her face.

"Not really but it's time for lunch can we go now." I asked impatiently.

"The doors right there, go for it."

I immediately got up and jetted through the door. I

got outside and stood by the door waiting on Farah so we could hang out a bit more. Everybody else went back to the courtyard getting ready to eat. I had my lunch so I too went and sat at the table with farah and we both ate.

" hey that looks really good." Farah said with amazement as she stared at the patty Tati had baked me.

"Yeah it's pretty good." I have an extra one if you want to try it.

"Yeah sure that'd be awesome."

I handed Farah a patty, she took a bite and her eyes glew really wide as if she just tasted heaven. She split the patty in two pieces and tried to hand me the rest.

"No it's okay you can have it all" I said as I moved her hands next to her tray

"Hey Joseph come play soccer with us." a kid from the field shouted.

"Sure ill be right over." I shouted back to them.

"Hey Farah can you watch my lunchbox for me i'm only gonna play one game." I placed my food down and tied my shoes a bit tighter and sprinted to the field to start playing.

"You ready, the game is going up to five! so make sure you try."

"Of course! I wouldn't be here if I wasn't going to try." I responded back.

The game started and I was really trying. Losing was not an option for me. My team mate passed me the ball and I ran for a couple yards, I passed the ball back when I seen him open again, then he took a low shot and scored.

"There you go." I shouted at my teammate and give him high five.

That's one up, the other kids weren't really expecting that from us. Couple plays later we were now up 4-2. One more goal to win. I was alone at the end of the oppositions field. I raised my hand and my teammate saw this and threw me a long pass on the ground and I first touched kicked ,and scored.

"5-2 who would've expected that. Me of course." I shouted and give a handshake to everybody who were playing on the field. That one game took all my energy. I was not looking forward to another game. I left the field and walked over to the table where I was recently sitting. Farah was sitting there and I was walking towards her. She had a huge smile on her face and was clapping her hands as I made my way towards her.

"Hey you were really great out there, I didn't know you were so good, bravo." she said as she applaud.

"Ehh i'm alright but i'm pretty tired now"

I took a sip out of my drink and got up to do a quick stretch.

"Hey wanna go for that walk up the hill now.?" I asked farah.

"Yeah lets go." she said

" Maybe we could go all the way up the hill where elizabeth's ghost is."

"Stop that's not funny." she said with a worried face.

"I'm just playing, but let's go for a walk."

"Okay sure."

Me and Farah made our way up to the hill, I made jokes and got her to laugh a couple times which I liked to see. She gave me a really positive vibe, I felt really comfortable around her. I didn't need to act different to try and impress her. And i'm pretty sure she also felt the same way.

"Hey we walked pretty far don't you think.?" farah asked as she looked down the hill to see how far we've came.

"Yeah we did we can head back if you want."

"Nah it's okay we came pretty far so we might as well go more."

"Hey isn't this the building where elizabeth went missing from.?" Farah asked as she dazed in the wods far from the building.

"Yeah it is." I responded.

"There's this song that if you sing it she supposedly appears, want to give it a try.?"

"Umm sure I guess, why not."

"Okay here goes, repeat after me."

"Elizabeth, Elizabeth come out and play, Elizabeth, Elizabeth if you're here show yourself. Elizabeth, Elizabeth come out and play, elizabeth, elizabeth if you're here show yourself."

Farah did as I did and responded the song word for word.

"Do you see her yet.?" Farah asked.

"No I think she's already here." I said.

"Hey I think I see something." Farah pointed.

"Are you sure."

"Click" a noise came from behind the building.

"Ahh!!." Farah yelled out, I too yelled and we both ran down the hill as fast as we could almost falling.

"What the hell was that." Farah shouted at me

"I don't know I think it was just a branch." I responded

" that was too scary we shouldn't have gone up there."

"Haha it wasn't that bad, tell me it wasn't fun."

"No it wasn't I almost broke my leg."

"sorry, we won't do that again, i'll admit that was pretty sketchy."

By the time we got back it was time to go back to class. There was about an hour left of the day before school ended. We got back to class and the teacher had nothing on the board. What a surprise I thought we usually have a bunch of work.

"For the rest of class you guys can get some drawing in, whatever comes to mind." the teacher said as she sat back on her chair.

If school was like this everyday I wouldn't mind coming here. I wouldn't wait all year on summer. I decided to draw a dog, i'm not the artistic type but I can get something done. I finished in about 15 minutes then rested my head on the table until the bell rung for us to be dismissed.

CHAPTER 4.

"Elizabeth"

Everything revolved around Elizabeth, she was the young ghost who haunted the school. Elizabeth was born in port-au-prince, haiti. Her house was just 10 minutes away from the school. Her parents were pretty successful businessmen. Most likely how she could afford to come to this school, which is a private catholic school. People said she was the nicest person you could ever meet. She would share her food all the time with the kids who didn't have much. She would bring in her toys from home so that other kids who had no toys could play with at recess.

Though Elizabeth was a really reasonable and nice person at school. At home her life was the complete opposite. She wasn't filled with the same life as she did when she was away from home. Her parents were really smart people and very rich at what they did. all that they believed in was to keep gaining knowledge. Her parents would make her study for hours on hours after she had got back from school. Elizabeth basically didn't have a social life after she came home from school. All she knew was school then goes home to read tons of books and study. But whenever she was at school she was as playful as can be. Knowing she would have to do more work when she gets back home later on the day.

Elizabeth was twelve years of age in the 7th grade. She had plenty of friends at school do to the fact that she was super friendly and rich. She enjoyed recess a lot, she enjoyed playing hiding and go seek, playing jump ropes, etc. Elizabeth had the same amount of enemies as she did friends. Elizabeth was the richest kid at the school, making her a target to being liked, also jealousy ran through other people's mind.

Elizabeth was pretty outgoing, she took whatever dare people through at her and was ready to have a whole bunch of fun. One day during recess Elizabeth and a bunch of other kids went out to play in the school yard. She first was playing jump ropes with her girlfriends. Then she got invited to go play hide and go seek with the older kids. She was resistant at first, she had this funny feeling running through her body. Maybe she was nervous because she never hung out with these kids before. She was already having fun playing jump ropes, but she ended up saying yes and went on to join the group to play hide and seek.

If you wanted to go hide and let somebody else seek you, you would have to wait for the countdown from three and say not it. She had screamed out not it but the other kids forced her to go seek. Everybody ran trying to go hide she seen most of the kids go up the hill were the abandoned buildings were. Up on the hill there were other classrooms that weren't being used. There was also old churches over there too. If you kept walking up all the way to the top it was like a dead end street with woods around the area, nobody knew what was behind those woods or how far deep they went.

She felt funny at first walking up there, she never went that far up before. That's where everybody else went to hide so she decided to follow. She walked and walked as she looked for the kids who were hiding from her. On her way up she had spotted two kids already and there only remained two more kids to find.

"Hey there's somebody over there." one of the kids pointed out behind the building.

"Are you sure, I don't really wanna go down there."

"Cmon what are you afraid of."

"Okay whatever i'll go check and see."

Elizabeth went down towards to building peeking over too see if anybody was hiding there. It was a really abandoned area and nobody was around too see.

"Chkk" the sound of a leaf branch being stepped on was heard by her.

"Who's there?" she looked around panicking thinking it's just somebody trying to hide from her.

"Okay come out now i'm done playing."

"boo "

"Ahh" she screamed then fell over the edge of the building that she was leaning against.

The other kids who were playing hide and seek with her weren't really close by and didn't hear her scream. They noticed that Elizabeth was gone for a while now and nobody could find her and the rest of the kids who were hiding showed themselves because they got bored of waiting on her. After noticing she wasn't coming down, the kids started to get worried. One of them sprinted back to the school to grab a teacher and look for her. But Elizabeth was nowhere to be found.

Some people say that Elizabeth was set up by some of the kids who didn't like her much. Also people say she walked too far up the hill and got lost walking into the woods. And there's some people who said she hated her home life so much that decide to venture off and run away. But till this day we'll never know the true story.

Over the years kids who go to the school talk about seeing a girl dressed with the school's uniform and a pony-tail standing by the woods. When they go get a teacher or point her out to someone there was no evidence. Elizabeth is still known as the young ghost of the school, she's been missing for seven plus years. A lot of stories surface on what happened. But we do not know for sure. Whenever we go by those buildings up the hill, We are to say this song and she is too appear.

"Elizabeth Elizabeth come out and play

Elizabeth Elizabeth if you're here show yourself

Elizabeth, Elizabeth, Elizabeth."

CHAPTER 5.

"Deputy Willot"

One thing is this and it definitely was a surprise. During the whole election of 2006 when Willot Joseph was running candidate for deputy. He was arrested and imprisoned for 4 months. Under false accusation by his malicious and unscrupulous opponents. But the population of maissade and inner city people believed in him. He finally won the election in two rounds. Despite his imprisonment he was elected MP for the constituency of Maissade with a percentage of 79% of the votes.

A lot of people stood against Willot during that election year mostly politicians and candidates. Since willot was a young kid he always took parts in the community. Trying his best to change the country for the better, and get rid of the nasty politicians who ran it. Willot always saw the bigger picture in his country and the people of haiti named him "The man of the people." the other politicians who ran the country in a way were always sitting on the people's money, living lavishly, not caring, or giving back. That is why willot ran for candidate to eliminate those type of people from the country. And finally give back to the people.

"Hey grab me that shirt that's hanging on the closet door." Djeny said to Mikah.

"Get it yourself i'm not your servant." Mikah responded.

I got up quickly looking out the window noticing it

was really sunny out. I wasn't feeling tired, I had a really good night's sleep.

'Isn't time to go to school.?" I shouted at my 2 sisters. "Why aren't you guys getting ready."

'No dummy today's the last day." Mikah responded.

"Yeah, Tati said we didn't have to go today." Djeny called out.

"Ohh." I mumbled.

"Yeah go back to bed sleeping beauty." Mikah said while laughing out loud.

No school, that sounded pretty awesome. I really wanted to say one more goodbye to my friends that were at school. Most of my friends at school I didn't see in the summertime. At the moment I wasn't feeling as tired anymore, I didn't want to go back to sleep. I laid back on my bed while staring at the wall noticing how fast this school year went by. Me and Farah were talking about how excited we were for the summer to come and all the fun things we would try to get done. I hope we could make it work.

" hey guess what?." Mikah whispered into my ears

"what..??" I mumbled

"Dad's taking us out today." she responded."He won the election and is deputy, all the false accusation is dropped and he's a free man for good"

"Whow that's pretty awesome." I thought to myself.

"Isn't that great Djeny."

"Yeah of course, Tati said she'll cook us some meals after we get back from the parade." djeny responded with a huge smile on her face.

"What parade.?" I quickly jumped up and asked.

"It's not really a parade were just going to ride around the city with Willot so his followers get a chance to see him " Mikah responded. "He's the most famous guy in the city right now."

"That should be fun, when are we going." I questioned with curiosity.

"We should be heading out pretty soon." Mikah responded.

"Hey Batista Tati has breakfast ready and she wants you to go eat right now."

"You guys all ate already.?" I asked.

"Yeah we been ate."
"How come you guys didn't wake me up.?"

"you been waking up early all year we thought you could get some rest." Djeny responded.

"Wow you guys actually care about my sleep.?" I asked sarcastically.

"Ha I would have woken you up early on purpose, I just didn't have the energy too." Djeny responded as she closed the door.

"Yeah I don't doubt it." I said as I went on to do my hygiene.

Tati wasn't in the kitchen when I was on my way to the bathroom, she's probably in her room getting ready. I brushed my teeth really fast and washed my face. I didn't feel like taking a shower since I showered last night.

I stared at myself in the mirror looking upwards since I was so short. I stared at my soft young face thinking of the day I could see my full body. I was always in a rush to grow up just because everyone treated me like a child, especially my sisters. I usually stood on a stool to see how my outfit looked.

"Batista come eat your food before it gets cold." Tati called out.

"Okay coming." I responded really fast. I hurried out to the kitchen table so she wouldn't get mad at me. She had made some scrambled eggs; with toasted bread, some orange juice, freshly peeled oranges and a banana. That was a awesome breakfast. I grubbed that food down to the last bite. I ate as if it was my first time eating in a whole year.

"Slow down boy the foods not going to run away from you." Tati said as she laughed. " I can fix you up another plate if you'd like."

There was no way I can say no to seconds on food this good. But she had washed all the dishes, and everything was put away. It would be hassle if I said yes. Besides I was full enough, I only wanted more food for the taste. I don't know what I would do without Tati, she's the closest thing to a mother figure to me. She made sure i'm always great, and tried to keep me in a joyful mood. She's one person i'm really thankful for.

"I'm really full actually, i'm going to change now i'll be out soon." I said to Tati.

"Okay boy go it done, i'll be out here waiting for you." Tati responded.

I hurried to my room to go change only to see that

my sisters were going through my shoes where my money was hidden. I panicked and quickly ran towards them in a angry manner.

"Why are you touching my stuff." I screamed out tackling Djeny and grabbing my money.

"Calm down we was just counting it." Mikah responded.

"I don't care it's not yours so dont touch it, what if I was going through your stuff." I said.

"Okay here you go kid before you have a heart attack."

I was really aggravated because they were going through my stuff. I have bad anxiety at times, it happens because of my OCD. when something I put in a certain spot is moved. I grabbed my money and put it under my pillow as I got dressed into some khaki shorts and a nice black polo dress shirt. What should I do with this money I thought to myself. I could give it to Tati that's the safest place to keep it away from my goblin sisters.

I got ready and went back out to the dining room. Tati was there ready and so was Djeny and Mikah. I had the money in my pocket that I wanted to give to Tati to hold on for me, but I wanted to do this without my sisters knowing. As we were heading downstairs to go grab my dad I quickly pulled Tati to the side.

"I got this from dad on my birthday, you think you can hold on to it for me.?" I asked Tati.

"Why you want me to hold it for you.? You're a big boy now." she responded.

"I know but I feel like ill lose it, and i'm scared Djeny will probably take it." I responded.

"I don't know what to tell you, that's sister and brother issue, you should be able to have that trust with your sisters and you should be able to keep your money safe, sorry kid." Tati said as she patted my head down.

Wow can't believe I just got turned down like that, I guess she was right though. I need to start building that habit of taking responsibilities for my action and my stuff. I placed the money back into my pocket as we headed down to the second floor. Dejny and mikah were looking out the window when I walked in. I had no idea what they were staring at, I ignored them and continued to walk towards my dad's bedroom.

"Willot are you in here.?" I called out.

"Yeah come in." Willot responded as he looked out of his bedroom with a toothbrush in his mouth.

"Congrats on becoming deputy again." I said as I gave him a hug.

"Thanks a lot big man, dad has a lot planned out for us, it will just take time. But everything should play out very soon." willot said as he gave me a pat on the shoulders. "Are your sisters down here too.?"

"Yeah there just waiting out in the living room." I responded.

"I should be ready in less than a minute i'll be right out."

Willot grabbed his dress shirt that he had on his bed and threw it on him. you could see his muscles ripping through the shirt as if he was about to explode, he was almost looking like a superhero. That's how I want to be when I grow up I thought to myself. Big, tall and strong. I left the room and willott followed after me. Just a minute after Djeny and Mikah ran to him, also giving him a hug. Now we were all here, finally ready to head out.

My dad had two cars, one SUV and one blacked out truck. I liked his truck more just cause of the size of it. I felt so high up whenever I was inside. Lucky me he decided to take out his truck today. It was the five of us that were going to be in that car. He had some other company but they were riding in their own car. They carried in the back of their car big posters of my dad's face on it. The other car had really huge speakers that were blowing music as we made our way to the city. One truck was in front of us and one was behind, following us the whole time until we arrived at the center of the city.

When we finally got to the core of the city there was a huge crowd of people screaming my dads name. "Willot, willot!" They shouted as they raised their hands up high, almost like they were praising him. Willot waved back to the crowd and he was smiling at his followers. Willot was standing on on the back of the truck and Began to give a speech. Willot talked about his goals and plans that he wants to pursue as deputy. He mentioned he wasn't going to use his power for his own purpose. But for the peoples purpose. He mentioned that he was going to be a huge help to the country even if the cost comes out of his own pocket. After the speech the crowd again went crazy and started to scream and shout. Willot had a bunch of T-shirts in the back of the truck. so did the other trucks. They carried water bottles, shirts, and some other utensils. The truck in front and in the back started to throw gear and other supplies towards the crowd. Everybody threw their hands up trying to get whatever they could. There wasn't enough stuff for everybody but it was a good amount.

We started to make our way back after a while. Willot said that he had a present for us . On our way back to the house there were still people on the side of the streets, waving as we drove by them. Tati and I had a box of clothes in the back seat with us. We started throwing it out to the car to spectators. It was pretty fun to be in a moving car and throw stuff out to peeps. At my age it was the most intense thing I've done.

As we arrived at the house, Tati started to pack the rest of the stuff that was left into the box.

"Batista help me get these things in the trunk." Tati said to me as she handed me a huge bag of shirts.

"Sure"

We put everything that was inside the car and placed it in the trunk of the truck. My sisters weren't doing anything like always. They already made their way upstairs and was probably watching us from the window doing work they were supposed to do. Thankfully we passed everything out and there weren't much stuff left back. Tati and I made our way upstairs, we were the only ones left outside since everyone rushed up. Tati had my dad's keys with her so she first went to his room to hand it to him.

"Willot, I have your keys with me, come out.! " Tati shouted as she knocked on his door.

"Give me one second" willot shouted.

Willot came out of his room talking on the phone.

The convo sounded very important but then he hung up.

"You could've put them on the table you know." Willott said to Tati.

"So that's the thank you I get for bringing you your keys." Tati said to willot.

Tati and willot never really agreed with each other. That makes sense since they were brothers and sisters. I can relate because I never agree with my sisters either. But even tho they argued. it was more of the "you're annoying me argument."

Tati went upstairs to the third floor but I stayed back with willot.

"Hey you know where we're going this weekend?" Willot asked me.

"I would know if u told me." I said sarcastically. I didn't like it much when people kept secrets or take long to tell me something.

"You a smart kid huh?" Willot responded. " but we're going to see grandpa and grandma"

"Wow really?" I said with excitement, I haven't seen my grandparents since school started.

"Yeah we leave tomorrow so get ready quick tonight."

"Okay I'll go do that now."

I ran upstairs to go tell Tati and my sisters what my dad just told me. I got to the kitchen and Tati was heating up some food that she already cooked this morning and was gonna serve us for lunch.

"Tati Tati, you know we're going Maissade tomorrow ?" I shouted.

"Yeah did your father just tell you." Tati asked.

"Yeah wait did u already know ? So that means Mikah and Djeny knows too." I asked feeling clueless. So everybody knew beside me I thought to myself. But whatever I'm going to get some clothes ready now. I ran into my room and my sisters were there getting there clothes ready. Mikah and Djeny were using this really big duffel bag that they would put there clothes in.

"So nobody was gonna tell me we were going away tomorrow." I shouted to my sisters.

"Oh we didn't tell you? It was a long morning I guess" Djeny responded.

" you should've read the signs a little bit, it was pretty obvious we were going away."

"Your bags right here, Tati said bring ten pairs of everything." Mikah said

"Alright" I responded

I started to search through the closet trying to find some outfits to bring with me. I wasn't too sure what to bring, I could bring some dress up clothes just in case we go to church. I need a bunch of shorts cause I'll be outside all day getting dirty. I need shirts too since I'm going to change if I get sweaty. I ended up grabbing 13 shirts and 13 shorts including some khaki shorts and a dress shirt for a special occasion. I also packed my slides an 2 pair of shoes. When I looked back in my closet I basically packed everything. Besides my dirty clothes I left my closet dry, I packed as if I was moving. But I rather over pack then not having enough clothes.

"Dude you're not moving you know, why you take so much clothes." Djeny asked.

"Don't worry about me,you guys packed your whole room into that huge duffel bag." I responded. " if I put my clothes in there it would be only a quarter full."

"Whatever kid make sure you bring toothbrush and all that extra stuff too." Djeny said to me.

"Okay." I said as I made my way out of the room going to join Tati in the dining room.

Like always Tati had a meal on the table for us too eat. She wasn't in here maybe she too was getting ready. I ate the food she had made for us while thinking about seeing old friends in Maissade. I finished my dinner and went into the living room, I sat down on the couch laid back, and put on a show to past time.

CHAPTER 6.

"Are we there yet?"

It was 8.00 am in the morning when we starting heading out to maissade. Tati had put away our bags in the car before I woke up. As usual my sisters were already up before me. I went and brushed my teeth and washed my face and armpit. I didn't need to take a shower since we were stopping at a lake on the way. Maissade was about 3 hours from port-au-prince. It wasn't a straight clear drive, we had to go up hills and down hills. We past a bunch of other cities along the way. The place I was more excited to stop at was Hinche. We had a relative who lived there and we'd sometime stop by when ever we went on a road trip. Plus that's where the lake was.

Hinche is a commune in haiti. There was a lot of people that lived there. I remember going to my relatives house and she'd take me out. Once we got on the street there was a bunch of people. Everything and everyone were filled with life. The color over there seemed brighter and the smiles seemed larger. There houses were more like cape houses or beach houses. There were a bunch of merchants on the streets, to the point where cars had to squeeze and drive really slow just to get by. Everyone tried to be different by trying to sell different materials to keep the competition level up.

Mikah and Djeny sat in the back of the car with me. I had the left window seat. Djeny was in the middle sleeping, leaning on Mikahs shoulder. We were on our first hour drive and there was only 10 minutes before we got to our relatives house. I was quiet the whole car ride

"Are we there yet" I shouted at Tati and willot who were sitting upfront.

"Yes boy we'll be there very soon, keep calm a bit longer." Tati responded.

"I'm hungry too, when are going to eat.?" I asked again.

"Can you survive 10 minutes ? you'll get all the food you want." Tati said as she looked back.

"You wanna stop and get some patty's ." willot said to Tati.

"Yeah we should stop I want some patty's." I shouted waking Djeny up from her sleep.

"Patty's ? I want some to." Djeny demanded.

Lucky us we were driving past a bunch of Merchants and there were lots of choices for us to get from. Willot pulled over on the side of the streets where other cars could go by. We all got out and stretched. My dad went across the street with Mikah and Djeny but I stayed back with Tati. We walked towards the lady who were right beside us. She had a long light blue silk dress on, with a wrap over her head trying to keep cool from the sun. Her food options were on a table.

"Bonjour madame" Tati greeted.

"Bonjour." I also greeted.

"How are you guys today." The merchant lady asked.

"We're doing alright, this boy right got hungry, we thought it'd be best to grab something along the way." Tati responded.

"Well I can help with that, I make he best patty's you'll come across and my plantains are the best too but today i'll suggest the chicken patties."

"Well we're in luck because that's exactly what we were looking for."

" how many do you guys need? He's a big boy so I'll make sure I get him at least two." The merchant said.

"We'll grab 8 please." Tati said.

"Of course." The merchant said as she started to pack the patty's into the brown lunch back. "That'll be 10 gourde please."

"Sure" Tati said as she handed the merchant lady the money.

"May I ask where you guys are heading ?" The merchant lady asked.

"We're on our way to Maissade but making a quick stop here in Hinche." Tati responded.

"Sounds like an adventure, I'm from hinche, and I'm telling you it's best that you grabbed food now because there's no way you would make up your mind once you got in there." The merchant lady said. "That's why I have my shop out here, I'll be getting customers leaving the village and customers coming in."

"Yeah that's smart, thank you miss, it was nice talking to you, we should get going now." Tati said.

"Very nice talking to you, have a safe trip now." The merchant lady said.

"Bye!" Me and Tati waved as we made our way to the car. Mikah and Djeny were walking with Willot and they too had food with them.

"We ready to go?" Willot asked.

"Should be." Tati responded.

Willot unlocked the car and we all entered.

Mikah and Djeny had some chips with them as well as fried plantains and fried chicken. Most of it were for Willot, but it was enough for everyone to share. I handed everyone in the car a party and I was left with three to myself. Willot told me to grab some fried chicken to eat and he also give me some plantains. We started drivin just 5 minutes after we started to eat. By the time I had finished my meal we'd had already arrived. We arrived at one of the houses that my dad had out there. It was a nice decent size house that we could fit in.

"We're not staying for long so you don't need to un-pack." Willot said to Tati.

"But are we still going to the lake?" I asked.

"Yeah I should have some clothes in here for you to use." Willot said.

Mikah and Djeny opened the trunk and found there bathing suit. I'm pretty sure they packed it on top since they knew we were going to swim. We all made our way inside the house.

"Whow, this looks better than our house." I said out loud.

"This is gonna be your house when you get older kid." willot said to me.

"Cool I'll take it." I said while smiling.

"How bout us do we get one too." Djeny asked

"Of Course I would never forget my daughters." Willot responded.

The house we were in was almost empty, it had basic things like couch and a bed and such. But no decorations or anything else that makes a home feels like a home. We stayed in there for about 30 minutes until everybody got ready to head out to the lake. We all got in the car and pulled off. Just within a 6 minute drive we arrived there. We all got out and started to walk. I was the first one running towards the lake until my aunt stopped me right before I fell face down the hill. The lake was at the bottom but it looked flat instead it was about a 10 feet drop.

"Boy you don't just take off like that." Tati yelled as she pulled me back towards her.

"Sorry" I said.

"How we even gonna get down there?" Djeny asked.

"We gotta climb down just be careful not to fall." Willot said.

The path that brought us to the bottom of the lake wasn't man built. It was going down hill and you'd have to be careful to not lose balance or you'd roll down. We got to the sand part of the lake and there were only a few people here. It almost looked like a private beach for us. There weren't any kids my age there so I'd have to play with myself or my annoying sisters.

My dad had a soccer ball with him and we kicked it around for a bit. My sisters were doing something with the sand but I didn't mind them. It started getting really hot so I asked my dad if he wanted to go swim with me. I wasn't the best swimmer but I wouldn't let myself drown and just to make sure I needed him to be there with me. I took a dive in the warm cool water. I stayed in for no more than 20 minute, splashing around and floating. I went back in the sand and relaxed in the chair. I had brought my marbles with me so I started to play by myself. I made a couple holes and placed a couple marbles, I tried to see if I can hit them into the hole. Marbles was my favorite activity so I played until it was time to leave, going back in forth in the water and marbles.. We spent about 2 hours if not more at the lake, by that time I started to get really hungry. We head out and went back to the house. There we showered and put on different clothes. Since we were already out here in Hinche and it was a couple more hours till we got to Maissade. Willot thought it was best if we got food out here to eat.

Willot said we should go to a restaurant and head out right after. We listened to what he said and we all went to the car driving around to find a good place to eat. We made our way into the center or Hinche and we found a couple restaurants but Willot decided we go to the one that he's been to before, he gave a good feedback about it so we all agreed. He parked his car outfront and we all headed into the restaurant.

There wasn't much people in there and it was pretty quite. We needed a big table since it was the five of us. As we made our way in a waiter came by and told us to follow her.

"This way please." The waiter said.

We did as she said and she led us to a family table for 5.

"What do you guys plan on eating today.?" The waiter asked.

There were a bunch of choices in the menu it was really hard to decide.

"I'll get rice with fried chicken and plantains please." Tati placed her order.

"I'll get the same thing she's getting" Mikah and Djeny said.

" can I get some white rice, with sos poi ,chicken and legume and plantains and a side of fried fish too. And get us all Coca Cola please." Willot said as he placed his order.

I looked at my dad with a shocked face because of all the food he just ordered. Then I thought to myself if I should get the same thing.

"I'll get the same thing.." but right before I finished my sentence Tati paused me.

"Don't mind him, your eyes bigger than your stomach. get him some white rice and some fried fish and plantains please" Tati made the order.

"Okay we'll get that ready as fast as possible." The waitress handed us our receipt.

$65 gourde was the price of the meal. We got a big order but they didn't take long to bring us our food. It's only been less than 15 minutes when the food started to arrive.

"Wow" I said out loud." I hope tastes as good as it looks."

"eat up boy and be careful of the bones."

You didn't have to tell me to eat twice, that was the only thing on my mind at the moment. I took bite after bite until I finished everything of my plate. Now I was officially filled and satisfied.

"Wow now I can agree he's your son, you both eat like pigs." Tati said while smiling at me and willott.

Even though my dad had almost triple the food I had, we fished at the same time. Mikah and Djeny were having a hard time finishing there meal but they put a pretty good dent into it.

Everybody finished to eat in about 30 plus minutes. Now it was time for us to get back on the road and make or way to maissade. It was going to be a long way. It was about 3 in the afternoon and I had more energy than ever. but as soon as we started to drive I started to doze and ended falling asleep all the way there.

CHAPTER 7.

"Maissade"

"Get up batista we need to unpack." Djeny said as she shook me trying to get me awake.

"We're here?" I jumped and looked around with excitement on my face knowing we just arrived at Maissade.

"Yeah and you slept the whole way there."

Willot grabbed the two duffle bags that he brought with him and put them on his shoulders with ease. Almost as if they were lightweight but they looked really heavy. My bag wasn't as big but it was harder to carry, I had to place it on my shoulders while I go through the gate and set it down on the floor, where Tati took it and brought it inside. Djeny and Mikah were both carrying their bags together and they brought it inside. I took a look around me and everything seemed so cool and good vibes were just all around. I took in a deep breath and immediately knew this summer was going to be a memorable one. Everyone else was already inside beside me, I was too busy taking a glimpse of the town next to the gate. The town looked a bit farmy, the houses were all nice, there were two main roads going straight and left. Never too much traffic happening here, everyone's local and knew each other.

"ahh" I yelled from something hitting me right calf.

"Haha." Kaptirin laughed as he ran towards me.

Kaptirin is my cousin, Willot's brother (Da) son. He was a knucklehead just like me, but I was nowhere near his level.

I was one year older than him but he seemed way imma-ture to just be one year younger than me. Whenever we were together just know that we were going to have the best time. My dad used to say he's a bad influence on me. Whenever he'd come over or we'd go visit I would get in a lot of trouble. But my uncle said I was the bad influence on him since I was older I should know better. But either way we always had good times and it was good to see him again. Neither of their opinion would change our friendship.

"That hurt you know." I shouted at kaptirin.

"You're just soft."

"Let me go make a slingshot and throw it at you and tell me if it don't hurt." I responded in a angry tone.

"Okay, there's some wood right there and here's a rubber band for you."

I took the rubber band from him and went next to a tree where a bunch of branches had fallen and picked out a branch. I broke it with my hands and shape it into a Y. From there I tied the rubber band around the stick and made my slingshot. I had to find a piece of cloth somewhere to put around the rubber band or it would break. Lucky me i founded one on the floor and decided to use it. It took me less than 3 minutes to make the slingshot. Once I was done I immediately grabbed a rock from the ground. It was small but big enough that you'd feel it. Kaptirin was facing the other way when I placed it into my slingshot. I pulled it back and shot it same spot he shot my leg.

"Oww " he screamed out. "I didn't do it that hard."

"Yeah it hurts huh?" I said as I laughed out loud.

"Ima get you back."

"You got me first so Ima get you back." I said.

"Whatever just make sure you look out."

Kaptirin didn't scare me much, but I didn't take his words lightly, he was pretty determined. Once he said he would do something he stuck with it until it comes true. But either way I would get him back and it'd go in a cycle I guess.

"I see you two causing trouble already." My grandma said as she walked out of the backdoor.

"Grandma!" I shouted then ran towards her and gave her a tight hug. "I missed you you know."

"Look at you getting so big already." Grandma called out.

"I turned 6 the other day so yeah you grow as you age right?" I said sarcastically.

"Yeah you're right, before you know it you'll be bigger than your father here." She said as she pats me on my head.

"Where's grandpa.?" I asked.

"He's our working right now don't worry he'll be back really soon." Grandma responded. "You hungry or anything?"

"Not really I'm alright we ate a bunch on our way here." I responded.

"That's good because I'm barely done with dinner." Grandma said.

"What you cooking?" I asked.

"I'm making rice and chicken today, usually same as always." She said. "That's the pot over there, the rice should be warm by now come check it out with me."

"Sure" I said as I followed my grandma into the section of the yard where she had all of her cooking materials.

Once we got there she had this ridiculously big pot that she was making rice in. it was the biggest pot I've ever seen. Next to it was a bunch of meat that was seasoned and were waiting to be fried.

"Is this just for us.?" I asked.

"No silly when ever I cook I cook for everybody In the area. Most people don't have money to eat so they come here and get a plate." Grandma responded.

"Wow." I thought to myself. "That's really nice of you." I said.

"Yeah gotta do what I can for others son, if you have enough for your own mouth full, you should always share with others who don't." My Grandma said.

That's the most honest thing that I've ever heard. My Grandma had a lot of sympathy for others and she believed in good karma. If you do good for others good will come your way.

"How long does it take you to cook everything?" I asked grandma.

"Not too long for all this food. No more than 3 hours. I don't rush since I will also be eating out of it." She responded.

"You should have a cooking business." I said while smiling.

"Nah i'm okay with what I do son." She said.

Wow I need to get tips on how to be humble from her.

She seemed so calm and at ease. I sat across from her and watched her cook for about 10 minutes without saying a word just amazed by her.

"Can you tell me anything about my mom." I asked.

"Sure son,what would you like to know." Grandma asked.

"Anything to be honest, I just wanna know if she's as humble as you." I responded.

"Well where do I start, your mom had always been a really beautiful young lady. When your dad brought her around for me to meet her I had told him to marry her because she was a keeper. She was always a smart young lady. But she wasn't raised with a silver spoon. She knows her worth and best yet she knew your worth. So she did what was best when she got pregnant, decided it'd be best that your father raised you. She knew you'd have caring parents, like your aunt and me she knew you would be raised how she wished she could raise you." She responded.

"Wow that's a lot to take in, but I understand thank you." I said as I went to give her a hug.

"You're young now son but I know when you grow up you'll understand and you'll recognize the sacrifice she made sending you away." "But don't you ever forget where you came from alright." Grandma said as she looked me in the eyes.

"Yes I'll keep that in mind ." I responded.

Willot came out the backdoor and rushed to where the food area was.

"You eating all the food without me." He asked sarcastically but almost sounding serious.

"If it was ready I would've." I responded.

"Ha I taught u well huh."

"Of course but you eat way more than I can, I still don't know how you do it." I said.

"Just keep eating , and one day we'll see who can eat the most, but for right now I take that trophy." He responded.

I had a really big appetite only because everyone in my family made the most delicious food. My aunt made food that i could eat for days on days. And my grandma cooked food I could never get tired of. It was great to have options. Either way the food would come out amazing no matter who cooked it.

"Go inside and fix up your room and get some long sleeves on, there's gonna be a few mosquitos out." Grandma said as she mixed the rice.

I heard what she said and immediately went inside to change. Bugs weren't my favorite things, if there was a way to keep them far, even just a tiny bit i'd do it. I rushed inside and unpacked my duffle bag on top of the bed I would be sleepin on. I took out a hoodie from my bag and some sweatpants that I packed. Around that time it wasn't hot out anymore . The wind started to blow and it was getting a little chilly. I fixed everything neatly and headed back outside. When I got outside I seen grandpa who just got back from work. He had a huge smile on his face when he seen me which made me smile more.

"Hey there kid, heard you were looking for me." Grandpa said.

I rushed and give him a hug.

"Yes I was, you've been gone all day." I said.

"Yeah i know, that's what work is you'll learn about that when you get older." Grandpa responded.

"Yeah hopefully." I said.

Tati was also out back with Grandma and Willot. They were all sitting down and conversing. Grandma and Tati began to fry the chicken, they had a bunch of paper plates out and a table set up right near the gate so people can grab the food. I got really hungry from looking at all the food but i held in my cravings. I started to get bored at all of the adult conversation so I went on a hunt to find kaptirin. He wasn't in the yard so maybe he was outside being a dummy.

"Can I go look for kaptirin." I shouted out to Tati and grandma.

"Make sure you're back within 20 minutes and don't go to far, he's probably across the street." Grandma shouted back.

"Okay be right back." I responded.

I left the gate and looked left it was pretty dark down that street. Plus I dint know much people down that way so I avoided it and went right. all of our friendly neighbors were on this side. Maissade was a small village but it's stretched out really far. The local people were the ones we knew best. I walked across the streets to one of our neighbors houses and kaptirin was there playing marbles with one of his friends.

"There you are, so you go play marbles and don't invite me.?" I asked.

"I didn't know you still played." Kaptirin answered.

"Yeah okay" I said as I pulled out a couple marbles from my pockets.

"i'm Joining in"

"Cool just make sure you don't lose." Kaptirin said while laughing.

"What are we playing anyway." I asked.

"Bloody knuckles." Kaptirin's friend answered. "If I win both rounds and get your marble into the hole you have to put your knuckles out and let me hit it with the marble."

"Yes yes I know how to play, you ready to start ." I said impatiently.

We set up 3 holes but they already had 2 other holes set up. We set the free marble in the middle and it was kaptirin's friend turn to go and try to knock off the marble. He took a shot and hit it on target but missed the hole and it slid right past. It was now my turn to go. I set up my shot and hit the marble but it slightly missed the hole and it was now kaptirin's turn to hit the marble. He placed his hand firmly and hit the marble and got it into the hole.

"Dang it" I said out loud.

"Show me your knuckles kid." Kaptirin demanded.

"Whatever." .

I placed my knuckles on the floor and kaptirin placed his hands also and shot the marble at my knuckles. It was the first time I was losing in marbles I'm not used to getting hit so it kind of hurt for the first couple seconds.

"That was a lucky shot you got, that will be your first and

last time." I said

We played on for a while. We went round after round, everybody rotating there knuckles from losing at one point of the game. The sun started to set fast and I had told grandma I would be back shortly.

"Kaptirin we gotta go, Tati said so." I demanded.

"You can go back I'm staying for a little longer." He responded

"Kid let's just go plus there starting to serve food, I'm not leaving without you" I said firmly.

"Alright hardo lets go, see you later T. " kaptirin said as he waved to his friend who then left as we left.

" I told grandma we'd be back in less than 20 minutes it's almost been 40 plus minutes now." I said.

"Yeah you gonna get a beating." Kaptirin said as he laughed.

"No I'm not because ima blame it on you. " I said while laughing.

"See that's not funny." He responded.

"I'm just playing, but we should be alright."

We got back into the yard and Tati and grandma had started to place food onto the plates and the huge light in the yard turned on.

"Where you two been ?" Tati questioned me. "nevermind that question just go wash up and eat ready to eat."

We both went inside and kaptirin went into the shower. I only had to wash my hands since I showered already and didn't get much dirty. I went back outside to hang out with Tati. Finally I seen my sisters who haven't seen all day, it was such a peaceful day without them screaming or nagging me about something. A couple minutes later one by one people started to come into the yard to grab there plate of food. I stood right beside Tati as she packed up plates after plates and handed to me to give out to the people waiting in the Line. Every time I give somebody their food they would say thank you and have a smile on their face. "Wow" I thought to myself. Now I get why grandma didn't want to charge the people. She much rather see somebody smile. To her that smile and thank you is the payment. That made a lot of sense since I witnessed it myself.

After everybody ate their food. The pot was about a quarter way to being done.It was now our turn to get food. Tati fixed me up a really huge plate of food, she did this for all of us, including kaptirin who just came out from taking a shower. I had only been here for a few hours and had already learned so much just being around my grandma and my whole family. There was so much more I wanted to know and learn and I wonder how long it'll take me to be as humble as grandma.

After we had finished our meal my aunt who was in hinche finally arrived here. With her she brought vanessa she was my favorite cousin ever, she was way nicer to me then my two sisters. She lived with us in Port-au-Prince but she's been away for a while now. She was a bit older too. Thirteen years old to be exact. She was also very mature for her age . Her mom is my dad's sister which made her my aunt. So now I had two aunts here again. They were both awesome I loved them both a lot.

"Hey Vanessa." I said as she made her way to me to give me a hug.

"Hey kiddo, what's up ."

"Nothing nothing just missed you a lot ." I responded.

"Awe i missed you too kid,"

Vanessa went to greet everybody else, my sisters were really excited to see her too. Now I was 3-1 but this time I had kaptirin with me and I knew he had my back so they couldn't torture me as much. I went to give Marilaine a hug. I was really excited to see her too. She was the one that always made me food before school and she'd always get my hair done too. She'd pick on Mikah and Djeny when ever they were annoying me. So I liked her a lot. Marilaine went towards grandma and Tati nannote to say hi and me and kaptirin were just hanging out by the gate passing time. Grandma fixed them a plate of food but there was a bunch of food left in the pot. I could've got second but I would've exploded if I ate anymore for the day. It was early but late at the same time. The time was 7 pm. There were a lot of activities going on but Tati would definitely not let us out alone right now. Besides she already closed the gate so we were stuck in here for the night. As long as I had marbles you can lock me up anywhere. Me and kaptirin found a spot in the yard and we began to make some holes and started our game of marbles. My sisters and Vanessa were together at the other end of the yard chit- chatting about who knows what. I didn't care much so I didn't mind them at all. And finally the adults were at the center where all the food was being served eating and sounding like they were having a lot of fun. It sounded like they were making up for lost time. There was a bunch of laughter that night we laughed and played until the stars came out and it was time for us to hit the beds.

Me and kaptirin shared a room and we basically stayed up all night talking about the most random things trying to see who could stay up longer. I ended up falling asleep first but i was determined to stay up. The day had put stress into my body and I lasted only an hour before passing out.

"Batista, you awake? hey kid you up.?" Kaptirin asked. " I won goodnight loser"

CHAPTER 8.

"Tallest Mango tree"

"Hey stop running so fast, you know we're out here all day right." I yelled as I chased after kaptirin.

"C'mon you just can't keep up." Kaptirin responded.

"Wanna bet?"

Kaptirin always wanted to make everything we did into a competition. We left really early that morning to go get some fruits. There was a bunch of coconut trees, banana trees, and some of the best mango trees around. We walked about 10 minutes before we got to the Forest where the trees where. It was really hot out that day. I wore a tank top, with some dri fit shorts that would let the air get to my feet. Kaptirin was also wearing something similar to my outfit. We both wore comfortable clothes for the weather. When we got close to the forest kaptirin wanted to race me to the mango tree. He claimed that the mango tree were going to made the sweetest mango's you would find around.

Me and kaptirin got to the mango tree and it was even taller than one of the coconut trees that were around. At the top you can see the huge mangos hanging on from the branches.

"You wanna go up first ?" Kaptirin asked as he took off his slippers.

"No it's alright" I said as I shook my head looking at the really tall tree.

Right next to the mango tree was a coconut tree that wasn't as high.

"I'll go on that one". I shouted." make sure you grab more than one mango"

Kaptirin looked back at me, then looked up at the tree and started to climb. He first wrapped his legs and arms around the tree. He does that all the way up until he got to the top. While at the top of the tree, kaptirin picked out 4 mangos and throws them down. I grab the mangos and put them into the bag we had with us.

"Coming down now." Kaptirin shouted.

Within a minute kaptirin made his way down the tree and was on the ground with me.

"Okay your turn." Kaptirin said.

"No way I'm going up there, beside we already have enough mangos."

"Are you at least going up the coconut tree?"

"Yeah that's what I planned on doing." I responded.

I give the bag I was carrying on my shoulder to kaptirin and made my way to the tree. At first I was nervous, it's been a while since I climbed a tree especially a tree this tall. I tried my best not to overthink the only fear was the height but I knew how to climb up and I was going to do it. I first wrapped myself around the tree getting a good grip. I climbed up slowly until I had reached the top and tore down 3 coconuts and threw them down to kaptirin. Going down was a little easier since it was gravity, I just had to keep a grip onto the tree. I got down to the ground and joined kaptirin who was stuffing the coconuts away.

"Ready to get outta here?" Kaptirin said.

"Yeah, but where are gonna eat these."

"I got a spot just follow."

Soon after Kaptirin started to run. I knew he wanted to race me there. I chased after him and we both began to run to the unknown spot he was bringing me to. A couple times I almost fell from running and jumping over branches that were on the ground, and having to doge trees. After a couple minutes of jogging and running we arrived at the spot,nobody won the race,it was a tie.

The spot he brought me to was a really big open field. There were rocks and spray paint on the ground it looked as if people came here before, maybe to play soccer. The field was mostly covered by corn. But they need some more time to grow before we could eat them. Kaptirin took a seat right on the ground where we were standing. He took out a mango and started to peel it.

"How do we crack this coconut.?" I asked.

Kaptirin grabbed the coconut from my hands and hit it really hard onto the ground. A crack noise came from the coconut so that was good. He took the coconut and smashed it again. A second crack noise came from the coconut but this time it was starting to leak.

"Here drink this."

I took the coconut from him and started to drink it. The coconut water tasted amazing. The coconut was already split so I took my fingers and split it into two pieces. I digged my fingers into the core of the coconut and started to eat it. I looked over at kaptirin and he already started to eat his mangos. Matter of fact he was down 2 mangos and there were only one left.

"Hey don't forget I want one." I yelled.

"First come first serve." He responded.

I walked towards him and took the last mango that was in the bag. It had a red and yellow looking color to it. It wasn't hard and it wasn't too soft. Once I started to peel it the mango started to bleed a little. I took a bite out of the mango and my mouth blew up with joy. It felt as if my taste buds were dancing from the amazing taste of the mango. I ate it as slowly as possible but it ended quicker then I wanted it to.

"It's good right." Kaptirin asked.

"Yeah but you had to be greedy and grab 2 for yourself and only 1 for me." I responded.

"Should've spoke up." He said.

"So you get to eat these everyday.!" I asked.

"Basically yeah." I come here once a day and pick out a couple mangos and coconuts." Kaptirin responded.

"Wow you're lucky." I said.

Me and kaptirin stayed on the field for a moment as we ate our fruit. The corn field right next to us was being hit hard by the wind and you can see it move back and forth. It was sad that not one of the corn was good enough to eat. I would've loved to have some fried corn right now.

Me and kaptirin finished eating and hanging out at the field and decided to head back to the house. We were gone for an hour. We started to walk towards the house, for some reason kaptirin didn't want to race me this time. Maybe it's because he ate so much and stuffed his belly up. We got inside the house and on the table was a big jug of lemonade. Me and kaptirin thought it was best if we grabbed a full cup each. I filled my cup a third way full and put a ice cube In it, I chugged the lemonade until my thirst went away.

CHAPTER 9.

"Church"

Sunday morning, it was really dark outside. It was only 6 am but the chickens and birds were up before everybody else. They were our alarm clocks in this town. Telling you to get up and go on about your day. I rolled around my bed trying to block off the sound. I wanted to get a couple more minutes of sleep in. I laid on my bed with my eyes closed overhearing everybody's conversations outside.

"Boom." The door opened. "Are you up yet." Kaptirin yelled. "You're the only one still asleep."

"Ahh leave me alone." I said.

"Grandma told me to wake you up so.."

"What time even is it.? " I asked.

"It's 7:30 now."

"Oh alright I'll be up in a bit." I responded.

Kaptirin left the room and left the door open. That was one thing I hated most. People not leaving things how it was. I think it was due to my OCD. When my things has to be exactly how I had it or I panic, and start to freak out. I rolled around my bed for a bit, then got up to close the open door. I opened up my window and took a deep breath outside. The air outside was really fresh going through my lungs. I posted my hand on the window side and stood there for a couple minutes just relaxing.

"Hey stop dozing over here." kaptirin called out.

I had a empty water bottle that was beside me I took it and threw it at him. "Stop being so annoying kid." I said.

I closed the window and went back inside. I went through my bag where I had my clean clothes, I picked out a nice shirt and shorts and a mix match pair of socks. For some reason I just couldn't find any matching socks at the time. I also took my towel and made my way outside where I would be taking a shower. The weather wasn't that bad outside so it wasn't too cold taking a shower. We had a pump on the side of our house and we had to fill a bucket up and shower there. We had privacy from the outside world but people living in the house could see us bath if they really wanted to. I didn't really mind much I just minded my own business and cleaned myself.

Mikah, Djeny and vanessa were all outside. They had already took a shower and were chit chatting about something. They were all dressed up really nice, nicer than usual so I was guessing they were going out. I wasn't the noisy type but if I wasn't aware of something I had to find out. After I showered I put my clothes on and deodorant and baby powder under my neck. I put my mismatching socks on with some slides and went on outside.

"Hey guys." I said with a deep smile.

"Hi kid! " they all waved back.

"Why you guys so dressed up." I asked.

"It's Sunday we're all going to church." Mikah answered.

Awe man why didn't I figure that out. I was overthinking it way too much. Obviously we're going to church it's Sunday. I looked down on my outfit and it wasn't church material so I hurried back inside to change.

"Bonjour Batista, we're leaving soon so hurry." Grandma said as I bumped into her.

"Bonjour Grandma, and okay I'll be quick." I responded.

I went into my room and hurried to pick out an outfit. I had a dress shirt by my dresser so I picked it out and threw it on. I found my pants in my bag of clothes and threw it on also and I put on my shoes. I was dressed neat but all I needed to do now is get my hair done. I had a pony tail but it was pretty messy. I knew my Tati or Grandma would not let me go out like this.

"Mikah can you help out with my hair?" I asked.

"Where's the stuff at, you know we're leaving right now so hurry up. She responded.

I had to hurry back inside to go get a comb and pomade that were in my sisters room. I had no idea where they could have it. I found the pomade on top of the dresser but had a hard time finding the comb. I looked all over but it wasn't there. I left their room and went into my grandma's room. I spent five more minutes looking around but couldn't find it. Only spot I could look now is my room, I hurried in there and first thing I found was a comb I brought with me from port-au-prince. It was right on the dresser. I took it and hurried back outside, when I got there everybody had already left to church.

"Seriously they really left me." I said out loud.

Me, Willot and Grandpa were the ones who stayed back. My dad was on his bed just laying down but he wasn't sleeping he was just on his phone texting. My grandpa was sitting outside frying some corn that he brought from his farm. He also made some grape juice too a big jug of it. He was looking bored so I decided to join him.

"Hey Grandpa, how's your day going so far.?" I asked.

"How you doing kid, I notice you got left back from church huh.?" He asked.

"Yeah it wasn't my fault tho, I was just trying to find the comb." I responded.

"Haha it's alright, that's how your grandma is, very impatient but she only left you because she hates being late and she knew I would stay back."

"You don't go to church.?" I asked.

"I used to but then people starting taking it very serious and I don't like all that pressure." Grandpa responded. "Besides its all about having faith and just like the church is a temple so is your body."

"Yeah Tati told me we go to church to praise god, and I really can't say no so I just go along." I said.

"Yeah that's good, your Auntie is a good woman." Grandpa responded.

"Yeah she's really awesome." I said.

My grandpa handed me a corn that was fried and looked really delicious. I haven't ate breakfast so I was really hungry. I took the corn from him which was still hot and set it down on the plate. He also had juice with him so I went and grabbed a cup and poured myself some. A couple minutes past and my corn started to warm up, then I grabbed it and quickly ate it. That was the best corn that I've ever had and I was craving another one, lucky me there were plenty to pick out. I took another one out of the fire that my grandpa was heating up and ate it. I didn't have much else to talk to grandpa about, the neighborhood was really quite since it's sunday. Everybody was at church or on the move. I was enjoying my grandpa's company even tho we weren't talking.

"Excuse me Batista, but Ima go sit on the porch that's where I'll be if you need me." Grandpa said.

"Alright I'm going to my room too, I might lay down for a bit."

"Yeah make sure you get out of those clothes too." Grandpa said as he laughed.

I guess he was teasing me since I got left behind for church and still have on my church clothes.

After grandpa left to go outside I followed and went back to my room. I changed back into the clothes I had on earlier. I found my shirt on the floor near my bed and my shorts under my dresser. I folded my clothes and put it back into my bag. I was really bored and didn't know nun else to do. I laid down on my bed and rested my head on the pillow, before you know it I was in the deepest sleep of my life.

CHAPTER. 10

"late night parade."

I was in my room when I overheard my sisters talking about going out to see this band that was having a private party in maissade.

In Haiti there were a lot of carnivals that a bunch of people went to. Instead of concerts and having it set at a certain place the carnival would move around. The person performing would be on a big moving cart and there would be thousands of people walking and having fun while they follow it around. Sometimes the carnival would move to about 3 cities at a time. I was really young at the time so Tati never let me go to them. My sisters were only allowed to go to the small parades. Like this one happening tonight in maissade. I knew there wasn't no point of asking since it would be a no. I avoided them and thought of another way to sneak out and go.

My sisters were really strict and followed through with what my aunt said. But sometimes they would be on my side and make acceptions. The parade was gonna be at a really big backyard that was next to a old church, it wasn't too far away. Vanessa was the oldest and she was going, if I wanted to go my best shot would be asking her. I waited till she was alone so my sisters wouldn't persuade her out of taking me. It was about 6.05 pm, the parade was starting in the next hour. Now or never was my mindset. Vanessa walked outside to the backyard and my sisters stayed in the bedroom and I knew this was my shot. I quickly hurried to her and tapped her on her shoulder.

"Vanessa I need to ask you something." I said.

"Yeah what's up kid." She responded.

"So I know you're going to the parade tonight and I really wanna go." I said.

" you know your aunt won't let you." Vanessa said.

"I know but if you advocate for me and say that you'll watch over me and you'll keep me safe then maybe she'd change her mind." I said in a sad tone.

"I don't know, and plus we'd have to come back early since you're coming along."

"You can only stay till nine anyway, so why would it matter if we come back together just a couple minutes early." I said.

"I'm not sure but I'll think about it and let you know." She said.

"Don't tell Mikah and Djeny they'll probably say not to bring me." I said.

"It's not up to them, but Ima talk to Tati and see what she says." Vanessa responded.

"Okay cool." I said.

Vanessa walked away and went on to do what she went outside for. She walked over to where grandpa was, he was baking some corn and she stood there and had a quick conversation with him. Grandpa handed her two cooked pieces of corn and she walked back over.

"Here you go that's for you." Vanessa said as she handed me the corn. "Oh and he said it's alright if we go with you tonight."

"You're joking." I said with excitement.

"yeah he said to stay close by you and don't let you off my guard." Vanessa said.

"Yeah I'll make sure I stay close by."

"I'll be responsible for you so don't let me down or I won't be able to trust you again." Vanessa said.

"Yeah I won't do nothing stupid." I responded.

"Okay we're leaving in a bit so go get ready, wear a sweater and some long pants for the bugs and so you won't get cold." Vanessa demanded.

"Okay will do."

I quickly turn around and run into my room to look for an outfit. I had these jeans I always wanted to wear but never found the occasion to do so. I think tonight might be the night for them to come out. They were hidden under my clothes in my bag. I took them out and put them on. I found a long sleeve shirt that looked nice and quickly put that on too. My hair was already done and I looked fine, I just needed to put on deodorant and wash my face. After I finished all my hygiene I went to go get Vanessa to tell her I was ready, she was in the room with all my sisters were and they were really loud.

"Hi!!." I said as I knocked on the door.

"Come in ba." Vanessa called out.

I walked in the room and they were all dressed up ready to head out.

"Why you so dressed up for.?"Djeny asked.

"He's going out with us tonight, forgot to tell you guys." Vanessa said.

"Really dude..?" Djeny said out loud.

"You know they'll be a lot of people right." Mikah said.

"Yeah I know, Vanessa told me to stay close." I responded.

"Yeah you better, I really don't wanna be responsible for you being lost or something." Mikah said.

"Yeah I'll be alright." I said.

"Okay when we leaving?" Djeny asked.

"We should head out right now to make it right on time, it started already anyway." Vanessa said.

"It's by the old church right? That shouldn't be that bad of a walk." Mikah said.

"Alright enough talking and let's make our way out there." Vanessa called out.

All of us were dressed up and ready to head out all we had to do was inform an adult we were leaving. We all walked out and went to the backyard where Grandpa and Grandma were sitting and enjoying a cup of coffee and chatting. Since Vanessa was the oldest she went on and told grandma what we were up to and when we would be back.

"Grandma said we should be back before 9:30." vanessa shouted to us.

"Alright be safe kids and keep eyes on your siblings." Grandma demanded.

"Yeah will do." Vanessa said as she waved.

Vanessa started to walk towards us with a smirk on her face so we knew that meant good news. I walked to the gate and opened it, Djeny was the first to get outside then everybody else followed. I closed the gate after I got out and we made our way towards the parade. Once we crossed the street and hit open road I started to feel the wind. It wasn't blowing too hard but it was enough for you to get the chills. There weren't much people on the road, our voices echoed through the streets as we talked and laughed. About eight minutes into the walk we saw a lady who was about to close up her shop. She was selling patty's, fried chicken and fried plantains, plus a bunch of good fruits. I had money on me and thought it'd be nice if I bought my sisters food, so I went for it.

"Hey you guys want patty's.?" I asked.

"Do you have money.?"Vanessa asked.

"Yeah I have some money my dad give to me." I responded.

"You still have that.?" Djeny asked.

"Yes I do, I save my money unlike you." I said.

"How much do you have.?" Vanessa asked.

"19 gourdes." I responded.

"so you wanna buy us food ba?" Vanessa asked sarcastically as if I was joking.

"Yeah I should have enough." I said.

"That's nice, but it's okay. I have money too I'll buy you guys something tonight instead."

We walked towards the lady and she didn't have much left on her table. She had packed up almost everything or she sold it all. She had 6 patty's left and some chicken and plantains.

"Can I get four patty's please.?" Vanessa said to the lady.

"Sure kids you guys are my last customers today." She responded.

Vanessa goes in her purse to take out the cash to pay for the food but the lady quickly interrupted her.

"It's okay young lady, those have been sitting there all day, don't worry about the money." The lady said.

The lady took the patty's and put them in four separate napkins and hands it to us. She then closed the bowl and puts away in her bags. Then she folds up the table and places it under her arms and carries on about her day.

"Be safe tonight kids." She called out as she left in a hurry.

"Thank you.!" We all yelled out hoping she heard us.

We started walking opposite of her and made our way to the parade. The church was less than five minutes from here and it was right across from the church so we were close. We walked and laughed as we enjoyed the patty the lady had give us. She said the patty's were stale but to me these were the best patty's ever. It wasn't too hot or cold. But the insides were warm. The crust wasn't too crunchy but crunched when I took a bite.

"Here it is." Vanessa pointed out at the large crowd of people.

" where do we have to be." Djeny asked.

"I guess just anywhere." Mikah responded.

The area was lit up very bright, the crowd of people stretched all the way into the yard. The church yard was also being used just because of how the area was formed.

The music was really loud and everybody was dressed in white. There were no more than 300 people but it felt way more. Being young and short made everything seem so much bigger in that crowd.

We listened to beautiful music as the sun set over our heads and we laughed with joy. At first I thought it would've been an adult party but there were also a bunch of younger kids there. The music was appropriate and we danced until our legs were about to fall off. I felt as if the music was touching my souls the vibrations were really right. All the peole around carried the same positive energy with them and the yard filled up with life and joy under the bright night sky,

The party was going to last until after midnight. But there was no way that we could stay out that late. We were having so much fun that we lost track of time and it was already five minutes past nine. I had my watch on and noticed so I poked at Vanessa and told her it was time to go.

" it's getting late." I said as I showed Vanessa my watch.

"Oh shoot you're right, we gotta get going." She said.

She passed on the info to Mikah and Djeny and we separated ourselves from the huge crowd and went into a corner.

"We gotta start heading back now or else we getting a whooping." Vanessa said.

"We were supposed to leave early anyway because of Batista" Mikah said.

"Okay let's just go then, make it there now or later." I shouted out.

Laurent Joseph

From here the house was no more than thirteen minutes away. The sun had already set and the sky was full of stars. It was a full moon that night and it felt closer than usual. We were walking in a rush to arrive, but not walking to fast or we might trip. I wanted to talk out loud to my sisters but they were having there own conversation and I didn't want to interrupt their thought. All I wanted to say was for us to stop and make a wish. There were so many stars out that maybe one of them would hear our call, and hopefully grant us our wish. There were a lot of things I would have wished for. But I wanted to be humble and having one wish would help me with that goal. I looked up at the sky and found the biggest star up there. In my head I wished to learn how to be humble just like ; grandma, Tati, my sisters and my mom. I closed my eyes for a second and prayed that one day I would figure it out. I grabbed my sisters hands and walked as we made our way to the house under the bright night sky.

Made in the USA
Middletown, DE
11 July 2019